PIONEERS

OF THE

OLD WEST

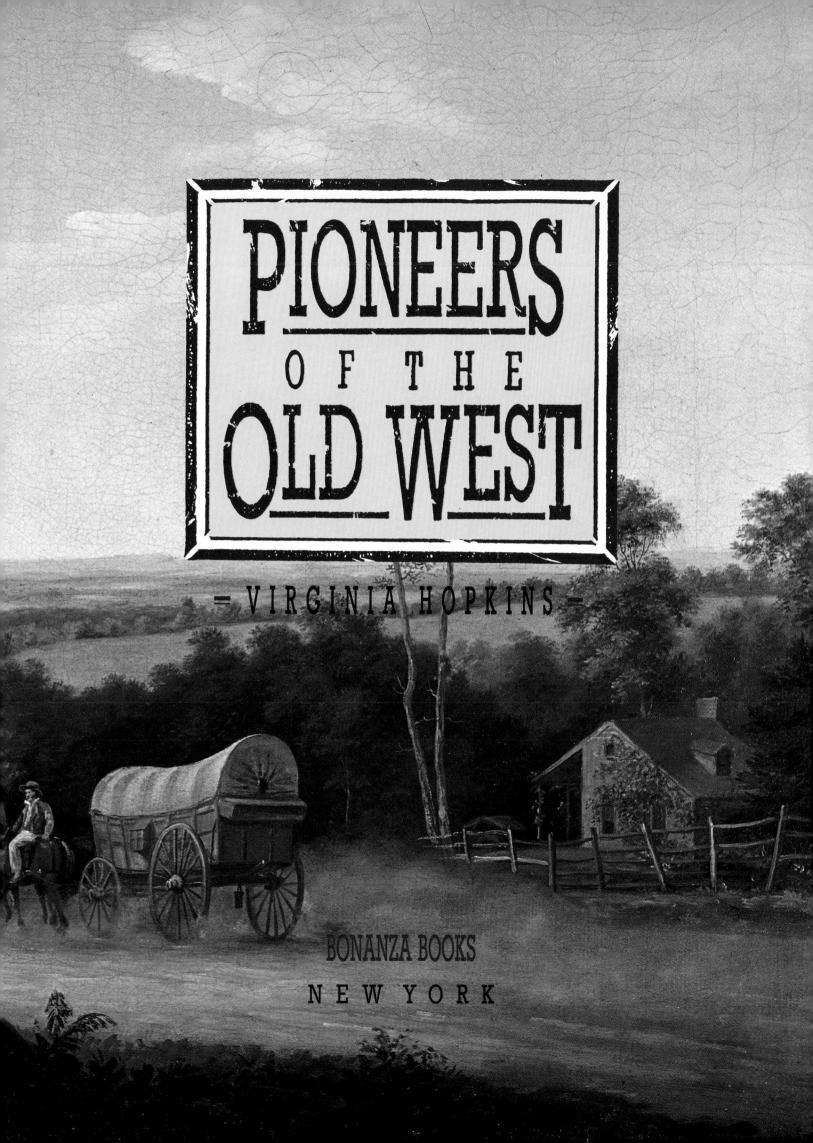

PIONEERS
OF THE
OLD WEST

= VIRGINIA HOPKINS =

BONANZA BOOKS

NEW YORK

A FOOTNOTE BOOK

This 1988 edition published by
Bonanza Books,
distributed by
Crown Publishers Inc.,
225 Park Avenue South,
New York, New York 10003

ISBN: 0-517-64930-6

h g f e d c b a

This book was designed and produced by
Footnote Productions Ltd.
6 Blundell Street
London N7

Editorial Director: Sheila Buff
Art Director: Peter Bridgewater
Designer: Ian Hunt

Typeset by Central Southern Typesetters,
Eastbourne
Manufactured in Hong Kong by
Regent Publishing Services Limited

Printed in Hong Kong by Leefung-Asco
Printers Limited

CONTENTS

1. The Settling of the Frontier West   6

2. The Trailblazers   27

3. Taming the Land   42

4. The Lure of Silver and Gold   58

5. Army Life, Army Heroes   71

6. Communication and Transportation   87

7. The Outlaws   102

8. The Lawmen   111

9. Women of the Old West   119

10. Religion, Culture and Jollification   127

Index   140

Picture Credits   144

THE SETTLING OF THE FRONTIER WEST

Emigrant families in covered wagons cross the plains and enter the Rocky Mountains in this idealized vision of the trek West, published by Currier and Ives in 1866.

The men and women who settled the American West during the 1880s were braving the wilds of the frontier for many reasons. Some simply sought a better way of life in a land unspoiled by civilization. Unfortunately, what they usually came up against were hostile Indians and the vagaries of mother nature. Many thousands of people were drawn West by the lure of gold and silver. They hoped to strike it rich and never have to work again. The vast majority of these people ended up using the skills they had in the East, whether that be running a grocery store, farming, or shoemaking. Of those who did strike it rich, only a fraction used their money wisely. Most went through their fortunes rapidly, in a frenzy of opulent spending, and found themselves broke when the dust settled.

It's safe to say that the frontier West attracted a great many misfits, malcontents, crazies, thieves, con men, fugitives, drunks, gamblers, and prostitutes. Perhaps these people saw the West as an opportunity to leave their past behind and start over, an opportunity to get away with murder literally and figuratively, an opportunity to take advantage of a lawless wilderness, or an opportunity to make a fortune by whatever means they could find. Those who were in trouble in the mid- and late-1800s went West. Women in fear of becoming old maids became mail-order brides. Young people who were disgraced, for whatever reason, moved West. Immigrants moved West rather than be stuck in an Eastern slum. Whether a person's intentions and character were good or bad, the West was a land of opportunity.

Politically, the United States government encouraged settlers to move West, for the more Americans living in an area, the better the government's opportunity or excuse for taking it over. Most often the army or navy moved into an area with the justification of defending American settlers.

THE NATIVE AMERICANS

The greatest tragedy of the settling of the American West was the near-extermination of the Native Americans, the Indians. The social and cultural morals of the era saw the Indians merely as a nuisance, as illiterate, godless savages impeding the progress of civilization. With this rationale behind them, most of the settlers, and certainly the United States Army, unhesitatingly massacred Indians with a ruthless violence hard to conceive of today. The intent was genocide, to wipe the Indians out and clear North America of their presence.

The irony of this tragic, wholesale slaughter is that the Indians had a varied, sophisticated, and ancient culture that in many ways held an emotional and spiritual view of the world far more civilized and advanced than anything the white man had to offer. There were dozens of tribes with their own distinct way of life and language. They could not conceive of the white man's concept of owning land. The principles of capitalism in general were difficult for the Indians to comprehend. Those tribes that weren't murdered were wiped out by venereal disease, measles, smallpox, and other white man's diseases. They proved to be extremely sensitive to alcohol, which has spelled the demise of many tribes.

In only a few decades, most of the Indian nations were shadows of their former selves. They were rounded up by the government and stuck onto land that nobody else wanted. The buffalo, which once

Cheap or even free government (formerly Indian) land (*top*) was a major lure for those heading West. This poster from 1890 advertises the benefits of South Dakota.

The Dakota boom (*below*) between 1878 and 1887 saw more than 24 million acres of land made available cheaply to immigrants. Gold was discovered there in 1875.

An adult male buffalo (*top left*) can stand seven feet high at the shoulder and can weigh up to 2,000 pounds.

Between 1870 and 1883 cheap rail transportation led to increased demand for buffalo hides (*middle left*) back East. Hunters swarmed over the plains, shooting the buffalo, skinning them, and leaving the carcasses to rot. By 1883, there were virtually no buffalo left to hunt.

numbered in the millions and were the mainstay of so many Plains tribes, were nearly extinct by the end of the century, wiped out by the greed of hide hunters and men under the illusion that shooting these stupid, lumbering creatures made them more masculine.

The Indian cultures might have survived more intact had they been treated with integrity. Instead, treaties were broken at the whim of the army, which pushed the Indians off their land whenever a group of settlers decided they wanted to graze, farm, or mine there. The lawmakers in Washington often believed that the Indians didn't have any rights to the land to begin with, and when the Indians protested, they were brutally and fatally reminded of who had the more sophisticated weaponry. One rancher and Indian fighter named King Woolsey called a group of Indians to a peace council

Rath & Wright's buffalo hide yard (*bottom left*), Dodge City, Kansas, in 1878. Forty thousand hides await rail shipment.

Shooting buffalo from a train around 1868 (*top right*). Indiscriminate slaughter such as this led to the near extinction of the buffalo.

Theodore Roosevelt (*bottom right*) was an ardent conservationist, who nevertheless shot a buffalo in 1904.

The Apache lifestyle (*far left*) was seminomadic. Crops were planted in the mountains in the spring and harvested in the fall; the rest of their food came from gathering and hunting. Infants were carried on their mothers' backs in cradleboards.

Pacer, a Kiowa-Apache chief (*center left*), photographed sometime between 1868 and 1874.

An Apache boy (*left*) with his face and legs painted, photographed around 1886.

The Apache people (*far left*) refer to themselves as Diné, the people. The six tribes of the Apache lived in what is now the state of Arizona. Their reputation as a warlike people is not wholly undeserved – Geronimo, one of the most famous Indian warriors, was an Apache. Here San Juan, a chief of the Mescalero Apaches, poses with a spear and shield.

An Apache bride (*center left*) in the 1880s. The six Apache tribes shared a common language and culture, but there were also distinct traditions within each tribe.

The main tribes of the Apaches were divided into several subdivisions. At the most basic level were local groups of anywhere from 30 to 200 people, led by a chief. This shot (*above left*) shows Nanay, a Chiricahua Apache subchief, in 1886.

The Apaches were hostile to whites in their territory, particularly after 1863, when the discovery of gold led to a large influx of prospectors. In 1875, the largest tribe, the Western Apache, were defeated by General George Crook. Many Western Apache later served as Army scouts. Here (*left*) a group drills with rifles at Fort Wingate, Arizona.

Navajo women shear sheep in this undated photograph (*top right*). Sheep were central to the Navajo economy, providing the wool for the famed Navajo rugs.

The Navajo people (*top left*) are closely related to the Apaches, sharing a similar language and culture. They did not have the Apache tribal organization, however. The Navajo lived in family groups in six- sided homes called hogans. Several hogans of an extended family were commonly located near each other. Further away, over the horizon, were more distant relations. This hogan and cornfield were photographed near Holbrook, Arizona, in 1889.

The interior of a hogan is shown in this photograph from 1903 (*bottom left*), taken on a reservation in New Mexico. The door of the hogan always faced east toward the rising sun.

Sheep are still important to the Navajo. Here (*right*) a shepherd keeps an eye on a flock in Arizona. With a reservation of over 15 million acres and a population well over 100,000, the Navajo are the

largest tribe in the United States.

The Navajo silverwork tradition (*top center*) is a relatively new one, dating back only to the second half of the nineteenth century. Here a silversmith poses with his tools and examples of his work in 1880.

The Navajos learned to weave (*bottom right*) from their Pueblo neighbors. Making a Navajo rug is a woman's job. She washes, cards, and spins the wool, and then dyes it using plants. Here a Navajo woman spins wool using a traditional spindle and whorl. Her loom is behind her.

In this photograph (*bottom center*) of a Navajo family group from 1873, a woman weaves at a loom; the man to her left holds a bow and arrow.

Conservation efforts have preserved a remnant of the great herds of American bison that once covered the plains. Today protected herds (*top left*) graze in national parks.

Chief Sitting Bull, of the Teton Sioux (*bottom left*), photographed around 1885. Absolutely fearless, Sitting Bull was a warrior by the age of 14.

Nez Percé Chief Joseph the Younger, sometime before 1877 (*top right*). Chief Joseph was the only leader left alive by the end of the Nez Percé war of 1877.

The last American Indian to surrender to the United States government (in 1886), Geronimo (*bottom right*) was a member of the Chiricahua Apaches.

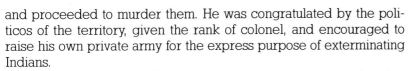

and proceeded to murder them. He was congratulated by the politicos of the territory, given the rank of colonel, and encouraged to raise his own private army for the express purpose of exterminating Indians.

The Indians had many heroes among themselves. Red Cloud, a leading warrior of the Oglala Sioux, was savvy enough to bargain with the white man and gain a reservation for his tribe that today spans most of South Dakota. The Nez Percé Chief Joseph was a brilliant fighter who led the Army on a wild goose chase all over the West in the 1870s; he won nearly every battle he fought. The famous Sioux Chief Sitting Bull inspired his men to victory at the Battle of Little Big Horn in 1876, although he was by then too important to

After their surrender to General Nelson Miles, Geronimo and his companions were sent to exile and prison in Florida. This photo (*left*), taken en route in 1886, shows Geronimo (first row, third from right).

Big Foot was killed at Wounded Knee. Here (*bottom left*) he lies frozen on the snow-covered battlefield where he was killed.

Casey's scouts (*bottom center*) plod back through the snow from the fight at Wounded Knee.

Chief Big Foot (*bottom right*) was the leader of a Sioux band camped on Wounded Knee Creek on the Pine Ridge Reservation in South Dakota on December 29, 1890. Sitting Bull had been killed just a week before. The Seventh Cavalry attempted to disarm the band, and fighting broke out (there is strong disagreement over who fired first). The resulting massacre of the Indians effectively ended the Indian Wars.

participate himself. He went to Canada after the battle, but was granted amnesty by the United States government and moved onto the Sioux reservation with his people. In 1890, at the age of 53, Sitting Bull was killed by federal agents for "resisting arrest." Geronimo was a famous Apache chief who tried repeatedly to make a reasonable peace with the white man, only to be lied to and repeatedly betrayed. When Geronimo finally surrendered for the last time in 1886, and his tribe was exiled to Florida, the Indian Wars were, for the most part, at an end. However, the Sioux chiefs Sitting Bull and Big Foot led an uprising in 1890 that became known as the Battle of Wounded Knee. At least 150 Sioux lost their lives in the battle.

The Sioux Indians of the northern plains (*top left*) were in conflict with whites from about 1850 to 1880. Led by such famed chiefs as Sitting Bull, Red Cloud, Crazy Horse, Gall, and others, they fiercely resisted white expansion. Red Cloud led a delegation to Washington to try to negotiate an end to trespassing through the Black Hills on the Sioux reservation by goldseekers. Shown here from left to right are Red Dog, Little Wound, John Bridgeman (interpreter), Red Cloud, American Horse, and Red Shirt.

Big Foot's band of Miniconjou Sioux (*top right*) in costume at a dance on the Cheyenne River in South Dakota in August 1890.

Rain-in-the-Face, a Hunkpapa Sioux chief, wearing a headdress (*bottom left*).

A bird's-eye view (*middle right*) of a Sioux camp at Pine Ridge, South Dakota, in 1890.

A tree burial (*bottom right*) of the Oglala Sioux.

When the Spanish conquistadors of the sixteenth century first saw the large, multistoried cliff dwellings (*top*) of the natives in Arizona and New Mexico, they called them *pueblos*, or villages. A better name for the civilization that built the pueblos is the Anasazi (Navajo for "ancient ones"). Anasazi culture reached a remarkable peak of sophistication during the period from about 800 to 1100. The three largest population centers during that period were at Mesa Verde, Colorado; Chaco Canyon, New Mexico, and Kayenta, Arizona. This photo shows the Cliff Palace at Mesa Verde.

Francisco Coronado (*middle left*) was the first European to meet the Pueblo dwellers, in 1540–1542. Beginning in the early 1600s, Spanish Franciscan priests tried to impose their culture and religion on the native peoples. The Pueblo people objected – and in 1680, they revolted. The Spanish were expelled for 12 years, but dissent among the Pueblos led to defeat when the Spaniards returned. The ruins of the mission church at Pecos National Monument are from a second church erected there in the early 1700s on top of the original church.

The Anasazi are the ancestors of today's Hopi and Zuñi Indians. In this photo from 1879 (*middle right*), part of a Hopi pueblo in Arizona and three of its residents can be seen.

Masked Mud Heads (*bottom left*) prepare to dance at Zuni Pueblo, New Mexico, in 1879. Spectators sit on the walls.

The Zuni Indians are descendants of the Pueblo people. Here (*bottom right*) pumpkins grow in front of a single-family Zuni adobe in 1879.

The Anasazi were primarily agriculturalists, raising maize, beans, squash, and other crops in the valleys. They developed elaborate irrigation systems, but a prolonged period of severe drought at the end of the thirteenth century led to the decline of their culture and the abandonment of many pueblos. This shot (*top left*) shows the interior of the upper ruin at Tonto National Monument in Arizona.

Religion played a central role in Anasazi life. Much of their religious life was based on the *kiva*, or underground ceremonial chamber. Here were performed rituals that helped the Anasazi live in harmony with their environment. This restored kiva (*top right*) is at Pecos National Monument in New Mexico.

At Mesa Verde the Anasazi built a circular sun temple (*middle left*). Pueblo life was rich in ritual.

Before about 1200, the Anasazi built their homes on mesa tops. However, attacks by marauding Indians led them to build instead on easily defended caves or ledges in the steep canyon walls. This aerial view (*middle right*) shows the upper ruin at Tonto National Monument.

Built of adobe or stone, the cliff dwellings of the Pueblo Indians were remarkable feats of construction. Each pueblo contained dwelling, work, storage, and ceremonial areas. There were no staircases; access to different levels was by ladder. Shown here (*bottom left*) is the first courtyard and the Spruce House at Mesa Verde.

Pioneering archaeologist and historian Adolph Bandelier (1840–1914) (*bottom right*) first recognized the sophistication and importance of the Pueblo culture.

A caravan of Mormon emigrants in covered wagons (*top left*), taken around 1879.

Two Mormon women and their small children (*top right*) pose before a building at Mormon Dairy (now called Mormon Lake), Arizona Territory, in 1887.

A store-lined street in Salt Lake City, Utah, in 1869 (*bottom left*).

THE MORMON SETTLEMENT OF UTAH

It must have seemed ironic to the Mormons of New England that many of the people harassing them had themselves fled religious or political oppression in Europe. To escape persecution, they moved west to Illinois and in 1838 created a thriving community called Nauvoo. Less than a decade later they were being persecuted again. When Mormon leader Joseph Smith was killed by a mob, the new leader, Brigham Young, was determined to find his people a remote place where they could settle in peace.

The Mormons began their Westward journey in a very methodical, organized fashion, with a smaller group going ahead to scout for land and places to create settlements along the way, and larger groups following. Brigham Young, in the lead party, headed for the Great Salt

Salt Lake City (*bottom right*) was laid out by Brigham Young in a grid pattern of streets 88 feet wide running north, south, east, and west. This formed blocks of ten acres each. The center of the city is the Temple Block, and in the center of that is the magnificent, six-spired granite Temple. The cornerstones were laid in 1853; the temple was dedicated in 1893. This photo was taken in 1908.

Brigham Young encouraged a system of church cooperatives, called Zion's Co-Operative Mercantile Institution, starting in 1869, after the economic isolation of the Salt Lake basin was ended by the arrival of the railroad.

Lake Basin because its reputation made it sound like land nobody else would want. In July of 1847 he looked down upon the valley and declared, "It is enough. This is the right place. Drive on!" By October there were close to 1,700 people in the new settlement.

The new land was harsh, and it took much community effort and dedication to build the dams and irrigation ditches necessary to make the area fertile. The challenge was to make the valley livable for the growing numbers of Mormons who wished to settle there. By the following year there were 2,400 Mormon settlers in the Great Salt Lake valley, and at least 15,000 more waiting to come. Land was distributed equally, and natural resources such as timber, water, and minerals relegated to public ownership. Many businesses and much of the agriculture were worked cooperatively and the valley grew abundant rapidly.

By 1879, Chief Joseph had been defeated and forced onto the reservation. This (*top left*) is the Nez Percé Agency on the Clearwater River in 1892.

Looking Glass, a Nez Percé chief (*top right*), on horseback in front of a tepee in 1877.

In 1855 the Nez Percé had accepted a reservation (*middle*) that preserved their homeland almost intact. In 1860, gold was discovered on their land; the whites demanded a smaller reservation that would exclude the gold fields. In 1863 a new reservation, containing one-tenth of the land originally set aside, was proposed to the tribe. Some leaders accepted the treaty, but others rejected it. Chief Joseph the Younger led a crushing defeat of a superior force of U.S. soldiers at White Bird Canyon in 1877.

Catholic missionaries also worked among the Nez Percé, to the dismay of the Protestants. St. Joseph's Mission (*bottom left*) was the first Roman Catholic mission among the Nez Percé. It was dedicated in 1874 by Father Joseph Cataldo, who had built it.

The Nez Percé Indians lived in the valleys of the Clearwater and Snake rivers and their tributaries in what is now mostly Idaho. Their first meeting with whites took place in September, 1805, when the members of the Lewis and Clark Expedition visited with them for a month. Soon fur trappers and traders entered the region. With them came Christian missionaries. From 1836 to 1874, when he died. Henry Spalding (*bottom right*) worked to bring Christianity to the Nez Percé.

Salt Lake City today remains the headquarters of the Church of Jesus Christ of Latter-day Saints (better known as Mormons), and the Temple (*left*) remains the center of the city.

Brigham Young (1801–1877) (*bottom left*) took over leadership of the Mormon church in 1844. He led the first group of 16,000 Mormons West from Illinois in 1846. On July 24, 1847, Young, traveling with an advance party, saw the Salt Lake valley and said, "This is the place." This statue of Young stands today in Salt Lake City.

Brigham Young had several residences in Salt Lake City, in part because he had more than 20 wives and fathered 57 children. This is the Lion House (*bottom right*).

The California Gold Rush, starting in 1849, brought thousands of emigrants through the Salt Lake Valley, increasing the prosperity of the Mormons, but also creating the beginnings of problems with the federal government. Brigham Young had stated from the beginning his loyalty to the United States, but he and his people wished to be left in peace to run their lives as they pleased. Anti-Mormon feeling was running fairly strong in Washington, D.C., and the government appointed non-Mormons to federal posts in Salt Lake City. In 1857 there was an armed clash between the Army and the Mormons. Eventually it was settled peaceably and the Army stationed troops in Salt Lake City. By the late 1860s there were more than 50,000 Mormons living in Utah.

The Shoshoni, Paiute, and Ute peoples occupied the arid area bounded on the east and west by the Rocky Mountains and the Sierra Nevada; to the south was the Colorado River, and to the north the hilly territory of present-day Oregon, Washington, and Idaho. Nomadic hunters and gatherers, they were well adapted to their harsh environment. Here (*top left*) two Paiute women grind seeds in the doorway of a thatched hut in 1872.

Four Paiute men (*top right*) play a gambling game in 1873.

Paiute children (*bottom left*) playing a game called wolf and deer in 1872.

The Arrow Maker and daughter (*bottom right*), Paiute Indians from northern Arizona, in 1872.

A Paiute Indian (*top left*) dressed in rabbit and antelope skins aims a rifle in 1873.

By the early nineteenth century the Ute Indians were known as daring horse thieves and crafty horse traders. This Ute warrior and his bride (*top right*) were photographed in northwest Utah in 1874.

The great Shoshoni Chief Washakie (c. 1804–1900) (*bottom left*) was noted for his commanding presence and abilities as a leader. This photo was probably taken in the 1870s.

Rabbit Tail, a Shoshoni scout, wearing bracelets and an ornamental vest (*bottom right*).

The next clash with the government came over the Mormon doctrine of plural marriage, or bigamy. Washington soon passed anti-bigamy laws and another clash was on. The political hostility and moral outrage of the rest of America was so great that plural marriages were disallowed in 1880. Soon after, Utah became one of the United States.

THE CONQUEST OF THE LAND

In less than a century the face of North America changed forever from a pristine wilderness to a booming civilization. The lives of the Spanish settlers, who had lived peacefully in the Southwest, and the

The city of Las Vegas began as a settlement by Mormons from Salt Lake City in 1855. Little remains except this old adobe fort (*top left*).

The Assembly Hall in Salt Lake City (*top right*) was built in 1880 using granite blocks left over from the construction of the Temple. It was designed to be a nonsectarian place of worship, and is still used as such.

Winsor Castle (*left*) in Pipe Spring, Arizona, was a Mormon ranching settlement providing cheese, butter, and beef to workers on church projects. The name comes from the manager, Anson Perry Winsor, who built and managed the fort starting in 1870.

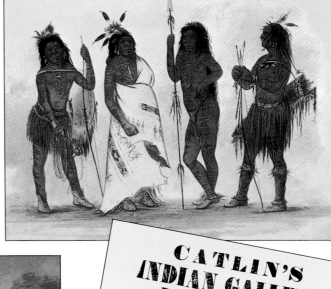

American painter George Catlin (1796–1872) was the first to systematically record Indian culture. In the 1830s he traveled extensively through the northern plains regions, painting the life of the Indians as he saw it. This painting (*top left*) shows the ball play dance of the Choctaws. The Choctaws lived in western Alabama and Mississippi.

An Apache chief and three warriors (*top right*).

Assiniboin Indians hunt antelope (*bottom left*). This Siouan tribe lived on the northern plains of the United States and Canada.

Catlin exhibited his works in the East and then sailed for Europe in 1839, where he lectured and showed his paintings for eight years. This poster (*bottom right*) advertises his exhibition and lectures in Washington, D.C., in 1838.

Big Soldier, a Dakota chief (*top left*).

Teton Sioux horseraces (*top right*) in front of Fort Pierre, South Dakota.

Two braves (*bottom*) with painted faces. At left, Massica, a Sauk; at right, Wakusasse, a Fox.

Winter village of the Hidatsa in Dakota Territory (*facing top left*).

Pehriska-Ruhpa, in the costume of the Dog Band of the Hidatsa Sioux (*facing top right*).

A Blackfoot Indian (*facing bottom left*) on horseback with a rifle.

Swiss artist Karl Bodmer (1809–1893) (*facing bottom right*) accompanied Prince Maximilian of Wied Neuwied on his journey up the Missouri River in 1833. His task was to provide a record of the flora, fauna, and natives encountered on the voyage, which he did in over 400 watercolor sketches of remarkable accuracy and beauty.

lives of the Native Americans, were dramatically altered. In the zeal for civilization, money, and power, the beauty of the land and the preservation of the environment were often overlooked. Mountain-sides were thoughtlessly stripped bare of timber for mines, homes, and fuel, creating erosion and mud slides. Buffalo and beaver were hunted almost to extinction, and the carrier pigeon was extermi-nated. The stench of frontier towns, caused by poor sanitation and slothfulness, could often be smelled from miles away.

By the 1860s Congress realized it had set in motion an unstoppable wave of settlement and civilization, and moved to set aside areas as national parks. In 1864 Yosemite Valley was declared a park, and in 1872 Yellowstone became the world's first national park. Soon after, the tourist business began in the West, and the former wilderness became a recreation area, as it is today, for millions of Americans.

The magnificent natural scenery of Yosemite National Park (*top*) was first seen by white men in 1851. The first tourist came in 1855; the area became a national park in 1890.

Yosemite Valley (*left*), the best-known part of Yosemite National Park, presents magnificent vistas of unspoiled natural beauty in every direction.

THE TRAILBLAZERS

Fort Union in 1833, as painted by artist Karl Bodmer.

The first men to venture into the vast unexplored territory west of the Mississippi River in the early 1800s were, by nature, an independent, resourceful, and courageous lot. Those who ventured into this unknown land, which bristled with hostile Indians, grizzly bears, and fiercely cold winters, had to love the solitude of the wilderness and the adventure of exploring unmapped country.

They went into the wilderness to trap fur, especially beaver. Later, when beaver went out of fashion, they went to guide wagon trains, but in truth they probably would have taken any excuse to wander through the great unexplored West.

With the exception of Meriwether Lewis and William Clark, this was not a literate group of men. They did not record their journeys, and the information we have about them is mostly through word-of-mouth. Tall-tale-telling was an honored pasttime among America's first mountain men, so it's hard to vouch for the accuracy of any of their reported adventures. On the other hand, there wasn't much need to exaggerate, either. Both John Colter and Jim Bridger returned from Yellowstone with tales of bubbling mud cauldrons and gushing geysers, only to be laughed off as liars. Those early reports of giant catfish in the Mississippi and monstrous grizzly bears must have seemed preposterous at first.

Thomas Jefferson had been anxious to send explorers West even before he became president of the United States. He had heard stories of the West Coast from those who had gotten there by ship, via the Pacific Ocean. His dream, and that of many American leaders and visionaries, was to find a water route across the continent. Their theory was that the Missouri River or one of its tributaries would be navigable to near the Continental Divide and the Rocky Mountains. On the western side they assumed they would find a navigable waterway to the Pacific Coast.

With this dream in mind, in 1803 Jefferson asked Congress to allot the money to send an expedition West. His bid was successful, and he immediately began organizing the trip. Just six months later, Jefferson completed the Louisiana Purchase, which, for a mere $15 million, added nearly a million square miles to the United States. The purchase included the land between the Mississippi River and the Rocky Mountains, from the Gulf of Mexico to the Canadian border.

LEWIS AND CLARK SEARCH FOR A ROUTE TO THE PACIFIC

A few weeks after the Louisiana Purchase, Jefferson sent his private secretary, Meriwether Lewis, and his friend William Clark off to the West to gather information. Officially they were to map the new territory, collect information on its flora and fauna, try to convince the Indians to sign peace agreements so trading posts could be built, and explore the possibilities of an inland waterway to the Pacific. Unofficially, the heart of the expedition was to find the inland waterway.

Lewis and Clark were old friends from the state of Virginia. Their skills, interests, and leadership abilities meshed perfectly. Lewis, born in 1774, was a captain in the United States Army, with a solid education and a keen scientific mind. He was known as an introvert. Clark, born in 1770, had bright red hair, and was an engineer, a mapmaker, and skilled at negotiating with the Indians. He was good

Soldier and explorer Meriwether Lewis (1774–1809) (top) was the official commander of the Lewis and Clark Expedition. He is responsible for most of the scientific information in the expedition's journals and reports.

President Jefferson tried to keep the Lewis and Clark expedition secret for fear of angering the Spanish. However, General James Wilkinson (facing bottom), who was involved in intrigues with the Spanish, informed them.

with his hands and experienced in building and handling boats. The Lewis and Clark expedition was one of the most successful in the history of the exploration of the Western United States. Much of its success was due to extremely careful and resourceful planning on the part of everyone involved. For example, much of the gunpowder was stored in lead casks, which were made into bullets when the gunpowder was used up.

Lewis and Clark carefully hand-picked a group of 45 men, and set up a camp on the Mississippi River to train them. About six months later the party began its journey by traveling upstream on the Missouri River. Sixteen of the men went only as far as the boats would take them on the Missouri River, then returned to St. Louis with the maps and specimens of flora and fauna collected so far along the trip.

The expedition's first winter was spent living in a crude stockade among the friendly Mandan Indians near what is now Bismarck, North Dakota. It was here that they hired a French-Canadian fur trapper named Toussaint Charbonneau as an interpreter for the Shoshoni Indians they would encounter on their journey in the spring. Charbonneau turned out to be lazy and worthless as an interpreter, but his Indian wife Sacagawea more than made up for his incompetence. She was cheerful, resourceful, and invaluable as an interpreter. She made most of the journey while caring for a newborn infant, who Clark later raised and educated.

As soon as the ice began to melt the expedition continued up the Missouri. By June the men could see the Rocky Mountains in the distance. The terrain became more rugged, and they met up with grizzlies for the first time. Lewis wrote that he would rather fight two Indians than one bear. In August they cached their boats and some of their supplies, and continued on foot. As they made their way into what is now Idaho, the men began to suffer from the harsh terrain and weather. Finally, they met up with a friendly tribe of Shoshoni Indians (friendly thanks to Sacajawea) who traded much-needed horses for articles such as blankets, beads, clothing, and mirrors.

The spectacular Buffalo Dance of the Mandans was painted by Karl Bodmer in 1833 (*top left*). Mandan society reached its peak in the period 1700 to 1750. In the 1770s, smallpox reduced the population to just 1,500. In 1837 another serious smallpox epidemic made the tribe virtually extinct.

The Mandan Indians of the Dakotas were famed for their spectacular costumes and ceremonies. Chief Four Bears (*top right*) was painted holding a spear and wearing a quilled shirt by Karl Bodmer in 1833.

The Lewis and Clark Expedition traveled down the mighty Columbia River (*above*) in what is now Oregon to reach the Pacific Ocean in 1805.

The members of the Lewis and Clark Expedition spent the winter of 1805–06 in tiny Fort Clatsop. The entire fort, now restored as Fort Clatsop National Memorial (*right*) near Astoria, Oregon, is only 50 feet square. It housed 31 men, one woman, and a baby.

The original Fort Laramie was a stockade owned by the American Fur Company and used as a rendezvous point by trappers. The decline of the fur trade in the 1840s coincided with the start of Westward movement by settlers. The fort, sited along the Oregon Trail, soon became a familiar landmark. In 1849, the fort was transferred to the United States government. This photo (*top*) shows the post trader's store in 1877.

By 1889, when this photo (*bottom*) of officers and their children in front of officers' row was taken, Fort Laramie protected not emigrants passing through but settlers who had come to stay.

Fort Laramie was an important military base,

serving as the command headquarters for campaigns against the Indians in the 1860s and 1870s. This watercolor (*top*) of the commissioned officers' residence was done by Lieutenant Charles Worden in 1887.

Fort Bridger became an Army post in 1858. Here (*bottom*) ladies, gentlemen, and children enjoy an afternoon of croquet on the lawn around 1873. In the background at left are officers' quarters; at right are the hospital and enlisted men's barracks.

Fort Bridger on the Green River in Wyoming was established by Jim Bridger and Louis Vasquez in 1843 specifically to aid emigrants on the Oregon Trail. This pencil sketch (*left*) dates from 1849.

Major Long holds a council with Pawnee Indians (*top*) in this somewhat fanciful engraving from 1823.

Major Stephen Long (1784–1864) (*bottom*) was sent on an expedition to the West from 1818 to 1820. One unfortunate result of his explorations was a map labeling the entire area east of the Rockies as the Great American Desert.

In October they came upon the Clearwater River, made dugout canoes, and followed that waterway to the Snake River, which led them to the mighty Columbia River. On November 9, 1805, the expedition finally saw the Pacific Ocean. After a long, hungry, cold, and wet winter, the expedition started back across the continent in March. By early September they were far enough down the Missouri to be meeting trappers and traders, who gave them the first whiskey they had tasted in many months. On September 23, 1806 they were back in St. Louis, writing letters to President Jefferson, who had long given them up for dead or lost.

President Jefferson made Lewis governor of the Louisiana Territory. Two years later, in 1809, on a trip to Washington, D.C., he stopped for the night at an inn near Nashville. There he was either murdered or committed suicide. He was only 35.

Clark was appointed Superintendent of Indian Affairs, with an office in St. Louis. Later, he was governor of the Missouri Territory and fought bravely against the British and the Indians in the War of 1812. He spent the last 15 years of his life as Superintendent of Indian Affairs again, negotiating many important treaties with the Indians. Clark had a good reputation for fair dealing with the Indians and was respected by them. He died in 1838.

MAPPING THE RIVERS AND MOUNTAINS

As Lewis and Clark were returning to St. Louis in 1806, Captain Zebulon Pike was setting out to make a map of the Arkansas River. He followed it into Colorado, where he came upon the lofty mountain eventually named after him, Pike's Peak.

In 1818 Congress sent Major Stephen H. Long to continue Pike's mapping work and find out more about the flora and fauna of the region. Long spotted one of the other highest peaks along the easternmost range of the Rockies, which was eventually named Long's Peak. Neither Pike nor Long got very far into the mountains or contributed significantly to the knowledge of the region. It was the mountain men, the fur trappers, and the traders, who were the real trailblazers of the West.

JEDEDIAH SMITH

Jedediah Smith was unusual among mountain men because he was literate and because he didn't drink, smoke, or curse. He wrote letters for others, and was known as a leader. Smith came from a New York family of solid Methodists, who gave him a strong religious background and a good education. In his early twenties, which was also the early 1820s, Smith, who was restless by nature, joined William H. Ashley's fur-trading company. He and 100 other trappers made their way up the Missouri River and then across the Rockies. In 1824, Smith learned of an easy route through the mountains from the Indians. The South Pass, located on the Continental Divide in Wyoming, became the major route for emigrants to California and Oregon.

Smith was physically and mentally a strong character, known for his integrity and courage. He gave his Bible as much credit as his gun for his many narrow escapes. He learned the fur trade in just three years, and along with two other mountain men, William Sublette and David Jackson, bought the Rocky Mountain Fur Com-

Buckskin-dressed hunters fire at attacking Indians on the prairie (*top*) in this engraving from 1853. The Indians soon gave up bows and arrows in favor of rifles.

Under the leadership of William Henry Ashley (*bottom*), the trading post system of the fur trade in the Rockies was replaced by a rendezvous system in 1825. Trappers fanned out into the mountains in the fall and remained there until the next summer, when they met to sell their furs, buy supplies, drink, and generally engage in riotous behavior.

pany. Smith had many harrowing escapes from Indians, grizzlies, and unpredictable Rocky Mountain weather. In one encounter with a grizzly, several of his ribs were broken, and his scalp was torn off from his left eye to his right ear. He had a companion sew the scalp and his ear back on immediately, and continued on his way. Smith was so badly scarred from the incident that he always kept his hair long to cover it.

In 1826 Smith led a trapping expedition to California, which was then a Mexican territory. He was one of the first Americans to reach the Franciscan missions in California, and was promptly ordered out by the Mexican governor. Leaving some of his party there, Smith made his way back across the continent, intending to map a direct route across the Great Salt Lake of Nevada and Utah, and nearly dying of thirst in the process.

A year later he returned to California to bring the rest of his party back East, but most of them were killed along the way. He finally made it to Fort Vancouver, a Hudson Bay trading post, and then back to the Rockies, where he began trapping again. By 1830 Smith had the foresight to realize that the fur trade was dying out, and sold his interest in the fur company. He was a good businessman, but his restless nature wouldn't allow him to settle down. He went into trade on the Santa Fe Trail. Just two years later in 1831, at the age of 32, he was killed by a band of Commanche Indians.

The restored McLoughlin House in Oregon City (*facing top*) is a clapboard home built in 1846.

Nobody believed John Colter when he told them about the weird geological formations he had seen in the Yellowstone region in 1807. The steam and spouting water of Geyser Basin (*facing bottom*) make the old name "Colter's Hell" seem appropriate.

Dr. John McLoughlin (*above*) was the chief factor of the Hudson's Bay Company in Oregon Territory from 1824 to 1845. Six feet seven inches tall, McLoughlin controlled the fur trade of a territory larger than all of Great Britain, extending a helping hand to all who asked.

The oldest and largest of the national parks (*right*) is Yellowstone; it was established in 1872. Most of the park is in Wyoming, although it extends into Montana and Idaho. Yellowstone is famed for its natural beauty and remarkable geological formations, including hot mineral springs.

In the course of an adventurous life as a mountain man, scout, soldier and Indian agent, Kit Carson (1809–1868) (*above*) guided John C. Frémont on three expeditions.

Kit Carson led a life that legends are made of – and they were. His daring exploits were first recounted in Frémont's memoirs. He soon became a popular hero (*facing*) for dime novelists, who wrote stories about him that were long on exciting action and short on facts.

JIM BRIDGER

Jim Bridger, who lived to the ripe old age of 77, was probably the most famous of the mountain men. Born in Virginia in 1804, he moved to Missouri with his parents and as a young boy ran a ferry to help support them. He also loved to hunt, trap, and fish, and supplied his family with much of their food. Bridger's parents died when he was 14. After a few years spent learning the trade of blacksmith, he headed West.

As a young man, Bridger was involved in many battles with the Indians, as the whites fought to gain control over the land west of the Mississippi. He quickly gained a reputation as a skilled trapper with a photographic memory for the territory he had explored. He was at home in the wilderness, and ended up living much of his life among the Indians. Though Bridger had a reputation for spinning the tallest tales in the Rockies, he was also known as a man whose word was good.

Like many mountain men, Bridger tried his hand at settling down. He founded Fort Bridger, in present-day southwest Wyoming, as an outpost and supply depot for wagon trains heading west along the Oregon Trail and the Overland Trail. He was so successful that the Mormons, who were settling to the southwest in Salt Lake City, stormed the fort and took it over. Eventually the U.S. Army took the fort back and leased it from Bridger.

Bridger served as a guide on and off for most of his life. It is not to his credit that he befriended and guided Sir George Gore, an enormously wealthy Irish nobleman who spent three years in the West slaughtering literally thousands of buffalo, elk, deer, moose, bear and any other living creatures he could find.

KIT CARSON

Kit Carson was one of 14 children in a family that moved to the westernmost frontier of Missouri in 1812, when he was about three. Though Carson was a very small man, with bow legs and a quiet manner, he made up for his size by being courageous and resourceful. He never learned to read and write, yet in addition to English, he spoke Spanish and a number of Indian dialects.

At the age of 14 Carson was apprenticed to a saddler. After a few unhappy years he ran away in 1826 and joined a wagon train heading for Santa Fe, 800 miles to the west across uninhabited prairie and barren deserts. From there he began his adventurous life as a trapper and guide, taking part in one of the first expeditions to California. He fought Indians, had narrow escapes from grizzly bears, and nearly died of starvation and thirst.

When he was 26, Carson married an Arapaho Indian woman he was "given" by a chief after winning a pistol duel with a belligerent French-Canadian trapper who had insulted her. She died, and Carson married a Cheyenne woman who seems to have divorced him after the way of her people – by throwing his possessions out of the teepee. By the time he was 30, the beaver fur trade was dying, and Carson became a buffalo hunter, supplying meat to Bent's Fort in what is now southeastern Colorado. A few years later in 1842 he was hired by Lieutenant John Frémont to guide an Army expedition to map out the best route West for settlers heading to California. Carson

The Santa Fe Trail (*top left*) on the west bank of the Missouri River at Independence. It led west through Council Grove to Fort Dodge, Kansas, where it forked, one route going southwest through the Cimarron Desert and the other continuing west into Colorado and then turning south at Bent's Fort. Both branches merged just beyond Fort Union, about 75 miles from Santa Fe. The trail was opened by trader William Becknell in 1821, and effectively abandoned in 1879 when the Santa Fe Railroad reached Las Vegas. So heavily traveled was the trail that the ruts left by the wagons can still be seen.

Bent's Old Fort (*top right*) reached its zenith of profitability in the period between 1834 and 1847. This pencil sketch, drawn by an Army lieutenant in 1845, shows the fort just before it became the advance base for General Steven Watts Kearney's invasion of New Mexico – a development that meant the end of the fort as a private venture.

The interior of Bent's Old Fort as it appears today (*middle left*) is little changed from some 150 years ago.

Bent's Old Fort (*middle right*) on the Arkansas River in southeastern Colorado was completed in 1834 by the trading

brothers Charles and William Bent and their partner Ceran St. Vrain. The fort quickly became a major destination on the Santa Fe Trail.

Fort Union as it appeared in 1860 in a watercolor by William Hays (*top*).

The interior of Bent's Old Fort (*facing bottom*) included workshops, living quarters, warehouses, and a billiards room.

Fort Union, strategically sited where the branches of the Santa Fe Trail joined, was an important way

station for travelers. The fort was so large by 1863 that it was almost a city in itself. Shown here (*bottom left*) is the Mechanics Corral.

John Jacob Astor's American Fur Company built Fort Union Trading

Post near the junction of the Missouri and Yellowstone rivers in present-day North Dakota in 1829. The post soon became headquarters for trade in beaver furs and buffalo hides with the Indians. The superintendent of the post was called the bourgeois.

The fort declined in significance along with the fur trade, and was dismantled in 1867. The bourgeois house (*bottom right*) remains.

Fur trader Manuel Lisa (1772–1820) formed the Missouri Fur Company in 1809, with headquarters on the Missouri River. He was the leading figure in the fur trade of the area, and was noted for his cordial relations with the Indians. This sketch of his home in Missouri Territory dates from the early 1800s.

was to lead three expeditions to California with Frémont, who said "With me, Carson and Truth mean the same thing."

When he was 34, Carson married again, this time to a Mexican woman named Josefa Jaramillo, and settled near Taos, where he raised cattle and horses. When he got restless again, he drove 6,500 sheep east from California and sold them for a large profit.

At the age of 44 Carson, who by this time had been made a colonel in the U.S. Army, was appointed to be federal Indian agent at Taos, a position he held on and off until he died in 1868, at the age of 59. As agent, Carson often served as the advocate of the Indians, and yet just as often he was fighting them. During the Indian Wars that were fought during the Civil War years, Carson was promoted to brigadier general for his skill in fighting the Indians in New Mexico. He was directly or indirectly responsible for the deaths of thousands of Indians, and is best known among the Navajo Indians for herding 50 Navajo women and children into a shallow cave and shooting into the crowd until all were dead.

JOHN COLTER

John Colter didn't head West until he was in his thirties, when he joined the Lewis and Clark expedition. Yet he was the first white man to discover what was to become one of our greatest national parks, and he left behind many hair-raising stories.

Colter was signed up with the Lewis and Clark expedition because of his skill as a woodsman and hunter. On the trip back, the party met up with two trappers on the Yellowstone River, who asked Colter to join them. He was lucky enough to be allowed to leave the expedition, and became a trapper. He later joined the large Manuel Lisa party of trappers as a "free trapper," which meant he could trap by himself, but he would trade his pelts to Lisa.

Before winter came the party built Fort Raymond at the mouth of the Big Horn river in Wyoming. Colter didn't much like the idea of being cooped up all winter, so Lisa sent him on a mission to search out Crow Indian encampments and talk them into trading at Fort Raymond. Colter had great success with the Crows. Finally, he

The Blackfoot Indians lived in the upper Missouri River region. From 1806 to 1855, when they signed a peace treaty, the Blackfoot repeatedly drove trappers and missionaries from their territory. This drawing of a camp of Piegan Blackfoot Indians near Fort McKenzie, Montana, was made by Karl Bodmer in 1833.

reached a village where they told him that if he went any farther he would wander into a terrifying land of evil spirits.

To Colter this sounded more like a challenge than a warning, and he immediately headed off in the direction the Indians had been pointing. This land was uninhabited and awesomely beautiful. Soon he came upon huge cauldrons of bubbling muck, pools of foul-smelling black tar, and geysers that shot 150 feet into the air. Colter had discovered what is now Yellowstone National Park. When he returned to Fort Raymond and described the area, he was accused of telling tall tales. This region, which he had allegedly dreamed up, was dubbed "Colter's Hell," a name that stuck until it became a national park.

The other adventure Colter is known for is an unfortunate encounter with the Blackfeet Indians. Lisa had sent him to try to befriend the Blackfeet. On his way to them he stopped at an encampment of Crow and Flathead Indians. There a huge band of Blackfeet attacked the encampment and Colter was forced to fight back with his rifle. The Blackfeet remembered him. A few months later, paddling down a river in a canoe with a trapping partner, they turned a corner and came upon 700 Blackfeet Indians. Colter's partner fought back and was killed immediately. Colter was captured and stripped of his weapons and clothes. The Indians gave him a head start, planning to hunt him down for sport. Colter's many years in the wilderness served him well, and he managed to outrun, and then outsmart, the Blackfeet. Unfortunately, Colter's encounter with the Blackfeet began a feud with the mountain men that lasted for years.

Ironically, after surviving so many adventures, Colter died in 1813 in Missouri of jaundice at the age of 38.

TAMING THE LAND

The dayherder keeps an eye on the grazing herd
on the LS Ranch in Texas in 1908.

It was the insatiable American appetite for beef, combined with the seemingly unlimited pasture of the Western plains, that created the character and the legend of the cowboy. As the gold and silver rushes of the mid- and late-1800s attracted thousands of new settlers to the West, many service industries grew up around them.

COWBOYS AND CATTLE BARONS

One of the most profitable service industries was supplying meat to hungry miners. Those in the meat business soon found that they couldn't keep up with the demand for beef. Meanwhile, there were thousands of head of cattle in Texas, and a low demand for them. Out of this need the cattle drive was born, and out of the cattle drive was born the real legend of the cowboy.

The American appetite for beef also created a handful of men who pioneered the huge cattle ranches of the West, becoming legends in their own time as cattle barons.

After three months on the trail, the cattle usually arrived at their destination thin and tired. The solution was to feed them for a month or two at their destination point and fatten them up. Out of this need sprang a new agricultural industry that grew corn and hay to fatten the cattle.

The era of the cowboys, cattle barons, and cattle drives had its beginnings just before the Civil War, but really took off after the war. During the war, most of the Texas cattle ranchers had gone off to fight, leaving thousands of cattle loose on the range to breed unchecked. By the time the war was over, there were hundreds of thousands of unbranded cattle in Texas. Many a demobilized Texas soldier, having nothing else to do, got himself a branding iron and a horse and became a cattle rancher.

While cattle in Texas went for around $10 a head, they were fetching at least $40 and up to $100 a head in the Eastern markets. The cattle empire quickly pushed north onto lands very recently occupied by the now-decimated populations of Indians and buffalo. Much of the land was in the public domain, leaving it free for any cattle rancher to graze his stock on. Between 1866 and 1885, hundreds of thousands of cattle were driven north in "long drives" along trails that have become famous in American history. These trails usually followed Indian or wagon trails; in spots they were 400 feet wide and eventually were worn down well below ground level.

It was the cattle drives that created much of the legendary lawlessness and gunfights in Western towns. Forty or fifty armed cowboys would come riding in after three months on the trail ready to raise hell and spend their money.

The cattle drives also made worse the already poor relationship between cattle barons and homesteaders, sheepherders, and small ranchers. The cattle barons often took the law into their own hands when things weren't to their liking, going so far in the Lincoln County War as to murder those who got in their way.

The most famous of the cattle trails was the Chisholm trail, named after trader Jesse Chisholm, who carved out a wagon trail from the San Antonio, Texas, to Abilene, Kansas. Chisholm was born in 1805 of a Scottish father and Cherokee mother in Tennessee. He lived in a Cherokee community and operated trading posts near Fort Smith, Arkansas for many years. It was said he spoke 14 Indian dialects. He

Jesse Chisholm (1805–1868) (*top*) blazed the Chisholm Trail, a cattle trail connecting the Texas ranches with the railheads in Kansas.

A thirsty cowpuncher comes to town in what is probably a posed shot from 1907 (*bottom*).

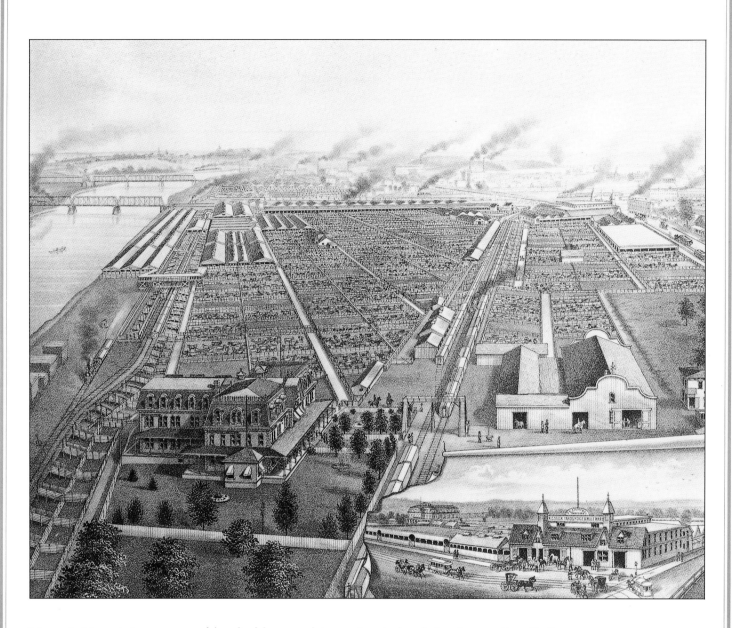

The cattle drive ended at the railheads in Kansas, where the trail-weary animals were fattened in stockyards and then shipped East. Note the railroad tracks in this bird's-eye view (*above*) of the Kansas City stockyards in 1887.

proved invaluable as an interpreter during federal councils with the Indians, because along with the languages, he knew the customs of the various tribes. During the Civil War he operated a trading post near Wichita, Kansas. When the war was over he created the Chisholm Trail to further his trading with the Indians.

The 600-mile trail became the main artery for herding cattle north. It crossed many rivers, but was still preferred because it was relatively level and had good grazing along the way. Between 1867 and 1871, more than 1.5 million head of cattle were driven north from Texas and shipped by rail out of Kansas.

The major Kansas cattle towns – Abilene, Wichita, Dodge City, Ellsworth, and Caldwell – were all located on a major railroad line. They grew quickly and frequently remained lawless for months at a time, giving them a reputation for the classic Western shoot-em-ups. In reality, there were thousands of people living in the cattle towns, many of them transients, and only about 45 people were killed during the cattle drive years. Many of those deaths were unrelated to wild-eyed cowboys, rustlers, and badmen raising a ruckus.

A little-appreciated fact is that many cowboys were black. In this rare shot (*facing*), a group of black cowhands gathers in Bonham, Texas in 1909.

LIFE ON THE TRAIL

The life of the cowboy on the trail has been one of the most romanticized aspects of life in the frontier West. While there is a certain
amount of romance in it, trailing thousands of head of cattle to market
over a period of two to four months was a hard, dangerous, and
uncomfortable life. The trails went through Indian territory; if the
Indians weren't paid a few head for passage through their land
they retaliated in kind. The settlers who were trying to raise crops
became more than a little incensed when thousands of cattle tram-
pled their fields or ate their winter hay. Irate settlers were as much or
more a threat than the Indians. The relationship between cowboy
and settler was like cat and dog – each side doing whatever it could
to provoke the other.

Weather was a constant threat. Between May and September,
when most of the trail drives took place, mother nature had all kinds
of life-threatening incidents up her sleeve. There were flash floods
that could turn a dirty brown trickle of a stream into a roaring torrent
in a matter of minutes. There were tornadoes, usually accompanied
by huge hailstones, that killed cattle and cowboys alike. There were
violent lighting and thunder storms, and at either end of the season,
blizzards.

By far the biggest danger on the trail was the stampede. Although
the herd was most likely to spook the first couple of days on the trail,
it didn't take much to set thousands of longhorns rushing blindly off,
trampling anything that got in the way.

The typical day on the trail began at 3 A.M. with thick, soupy ranch
coffee and some kind of basic grub for breakfast. The cook was the
most important member of any trail drive, next to the trail boss.
Cowboys were willing to put up with a lot of hardship, but they
weren't willing to put up with bad grub. The herd was generally

Branding calves (*top*)
on a windy day at the JR
Ranch in Texas, 1907.

A more efficient way to
brand cattle was to herd
them through a chute into
the branding area, as these
cowboys (*bottom*) are
doing on the Shoe Bar
Ranch in Texas in 1905.

Chow time on the trail (*above*). The cowboys sit among their bedrolls near a typical buckboard-style chuckwagon.

A cook for the LS Ranch in Texas (*right*) mixes biscuits at the business end of a chuckwagon.

Dust on the drags (*facing top*). The cowboys bringing up the rear of the herd would be literally caked in dust at the end of the day.

Most cowboys did not own their horses. Instead, they were supplied by their employers. On the trail a cowboy needed at least two horses a day. A cowboy called a (*facing bottom left*) wrangler was detailed to take care of the horses, kept in a rope corral called a remuda.

Keeping the herd together was of paramount importance. Here (*facing bottom right*) two cowboys on the OR Ranch in Arizona rope an outlaw steer.

moving before sunup, led by men in the front called pointers. Then came flank riders, and bringing up the rear, eating all the dust, came the drag riders. The cattle were moved along at a slow, steady pace that allowed them some grazing. In the late morning there was a lunch break for the men, and a siesta for the cattle. After a few hours' rest, the outfit got moving again and pushed along until evening, when the cattle were given grazing time. Ideally, the drives were planned so that there were water holes at the end of each day.

A trail boss or foreman on a long trail drive usually stood to make good money from it, providing he arrived at his destination with most of his cattle intact and reasonably well fed. The cowboy rarely made much money, and what he did make was usually spent on whiskey and women at the end of the trail.

THE CATTLE BARONS

The first man to move cattle north from Texas was Oliver Loving, who was born in Kentucky in 1812. When he was in his early thirties he moved with his wife to Collin County, Texas, where they were homesteaders for nearly a decade. In 1856 Loving became involved in the cattle industry, and three years later became the first rancher to drive his cattle to the Chicago yards, establishing what became known as the Shawnee Trail.

Cattlemen contemptuously referred to settlers as "nesters," and tried to drive them off the range. This nester family (*facing top*) was photographed on the range of the Three Block Ranch near Richardson, New Mexico, around 1905.

A cowboy needed more than one well-trained horse. Breaking and training mounts was an important part of a cowboy's work. Here (*facing middle*) a cowboy ropes a saddled but unbroken horse preparatory to mounting.

The next step is to mount the horse and attempt to stay on – a risky business, as this cowboy (*facing bottom*) from the LS Ranch in Texas learns.

When the Civil War began Loving supplied the Confederates with beef. After the war he went into business with a former Indian scout named Charles Goodnight. In 1866, Loving and Goodnight drove a herd to the South Platte River north of Denver, establishing a trail that became known as the Goodnight – Loving Trail. Unfortunately, the partnership didn't last very long, because Loving was wounded by a Commanche arrow in 1867, and died of gangrene three weeks later.

Of necessity, cowboys were self-sufficient sorts. Some developed rough-and-ready skills in doctoring – cows, horses, and men – while others (*above*) provided that essential service, haircuts.

Being a cowboy was hard, dirty, low-paying, and often dangerous work. Here (*left*) cowboys of the Turkey Tracks Ranch come to the aid of a buddy whose mount has stepped in a prairie dog hole and thrown him.

Blizzards (*above*) were another serious problem on the range – both cattle and cowboys could freeze to death.

Weather was a constant threat to the cowboy. Here (*left*) a massive dust storm passes over Midland, Texas in 1894.

Fort Concho was founded in 1867 and became an organizing point near the start of the Goodnight–Loving Trail. Between 1875 and 1892, the fort also served as headquarters for Colonel Benjamin Grierson's 10th Cavalry, an elite unit of black troops. This view of the parade ground and barracks (*facing top*) dates from the 1870s.

Colonel Ranald S. Mackenzie (*facing bottom*) was post commander of Fort Concho during the 1870s.

It is said that his dying words were, "Don't leave me in foreign soil, take me back to Texas."

Goodnight continued to drive cattle, at one point working with the New Mexico cattle baron John Chisum. After moving cattle around the West for nearly a decade, Goodnight settled into the JA Ranch on the Texas panhandle, in partnership with John G. Adair. The two of them prospered, creating one of the largest ranches in Texas – at one point they were grazing 100,000 cattle on a million acres of range. Goodnight was instrumental in improving Texas cattle, by introducing Hereford bulls to his herds. Goodnight finally sold his share in the ranch to Adair's widow Cornelia in 1890. He continued to run a small ranch in the Texas Panhandle until his death in 1929.

John S. "Jinglebob" Chisum (not to be confused with Jesse Chisholm and the Chisholm Trail) was a New Mexico cattle baron. He was born in 1824 in Tennessee, and moved to Paris, Texas with his parents when he was a teenager. He was well on his way to becoming a cattle baron by the time he was in his early thirties. At that time he decided to push farther west with his herd of 10,000, becoming the first large American cattle rancher to settle in northeastern New Mexico. By 1875 he had 80,000 cattle and employed 100 cowboys.

Chisum was known as "Jinglebob John" after his brand, which was an earmark that split the ear so that the lower part of it drooped. He was somewhat notorious for taking the law into his own hands, and

Cattle from one ranch often wandered into the herds of another. Here (*facing top*) a cowboy called a stray man rides through a herd on round-up day, looking for cattle from his ranch.

A day herder (*facing top*) relaxes in the saddle while keeping an eye on the grazing herd at the LS Ranch, Texas, in 1908.

ruled a good deal of New Mexico with a small army of well-armed cowboys. Chisum was one of the cattle barons who became involved in the often deadly cattle wars, which pitted small cattle ranchers, sheepherders, and homesteaders against the barons, who threatened to swallow the stock of the smaller outfits, fence off grazing land so sheep couldn't get to it, and trample the land of settlers. In turn, it seems likely that these groups also relieved Chisum of many thousands of cattle.

Jinglebob John never married. The domestic side of his South Spring Ranch was tended to by his niece Sally Chisum. Uncle John was a friend of Billy the Kid, who apparently took a shine to Sally and had an affair with her. It is her reminiscences that have supplied historians with descriptions of many of the famous outlaws of the day, including Pat Garrett.

Samuel Maverick was a lawyer who unintentionally became a cattle baron. Before the Civil War he reluctantly accepted a herd of cattle as payment of a debt, and left them on a Texas island in the charge of a caretaker. He returned eight years later to find that many of his cattle had wandered off the island via a sandbar, and that very few of his now thousands of cattle bore his MS brand. Maverick drove his herd off the island and sold it. Since his original herd of 400 had turned into thousands over the years, his neighbors often assumed that any unbranded animal belonged to him, and they began referring to unbranded animals in general as "mavericks." Mavericking also became a synonym for rustling, and later came to mean a person who kept apart from the crowd, or who was different.

In 1867 Charles Goodnight (1836–1929) (*left*) decided he could get a better price for his cattle in New Mexico than he could in Texas. With his partner Oliver Loving he marked a trail from Fort Belknap, Texas, to Fort Sumner, New Mexico. This route, known as the Goodnight–Loving Trail, became one of the most heavily traveled cattle trails in the Southwest.

Samuel Maverick (*right*) was an unintentional cattle baron. He left behind a herd of cattle when he went off to fight in the Civil War. When he returned, his small herd had grown into a large herd of thousands of unbranded cattle.

THE KING RANCH

Richard King (1824–1885), born of poor Irish parents in New York City, eventually accumulated 1.27 million acres of Texas ranchland. Grazing on his land at any given time were 40,000 cattle and over 6,000 horses.

The story of the King Ranch is one of the great success stories of Texas ranching. This huge spread was started in 1852 by Colonel Richard King. Today it stretches over one million acres, and supports over 150,000 head of cattle and horses.

Richard King was born in 1824 in the slums of New York City, the son of very poor Irish immigrants. Life at home was so bad that King ran away at the age of 13, stowing away on a freighter bound for the Gulf of Mexico. King was ambitious from an early age. During his teenage years he worked around the docks of the Southern waterways, eventually earning a pilot's license and becoming an expert in the steamboat freight business. In his twenties King went into the riverboat business with partner Mifflin Kenedy, and by 1846 had a fleet of 22 boats.

By the time he was in his early forties, King had a nice nest egg, and was secure in the riverboat business. He was ready for new challenges, and decided to try his hand at ranching. In 1853 he dis-

Joseph Farwell Glidden, a farmer from DeKalb, Illinois, invented barbed wire in 1873. This inexpensive, practical fencing led to revolutionary changes in the West. The open range was fenced even as the railheads were brought ever closer to cattle country. The two events brought the era of the massive cattle drive to an end.

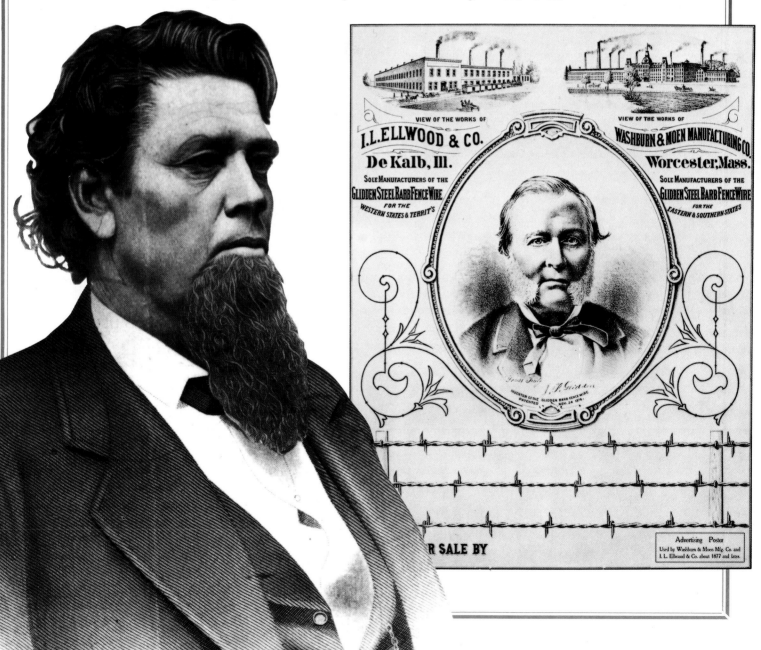

VIEW OF THE WORKS OF
I.L. ELLWOOD & CO.
De Kalb, Ill.
SOLE MANUFACTURERS OF THE
GLIDDEN STEEL BARB FENCE WIRE
FOR THE
WESTERN STATES & TERRIT'S

VIEW OF THE WORKS OF
WASHBURN & MOEN MANUFACTURING CO.
Worcester, Mass.
SOLE MANUFACTURERS OF THE
GLIDDEN STEEL BARB FENCE WIRE
FOR THE
EASTERN & SOUTHERN STATES

INVENTOR OF THE GLIDDEN BARB FENCE WIRE.
PATENTED NOV. 24, 1874.

FOR SALE BY

Advertising Poster
Used by Washburn & Moen Mfg. Co. and
I. L. Ellwood & Co. about 1877 and later.

covered a beautiful parcel of 15,500 acres on the Santa Getrudis Creek in southern Texas, found the owners of the original Spanish land grant, and paid them $300 for it. Not long after he bought an adjacent parcel of 53,000 acres of prime grassland, and he had the beginnings of a Texas ranch. King's first partner in this venture was a one-time Texas Ranger named Gideon Lewis, better known as Legs Lewis. Legs was to run the operation on a day-to-day basis, so that King could continue to run the riverboat business and pay for the ranch in its formative years.

King went about developing his ranch in a carefully considered, methodical manner. This care would carry him through droughts, depressions, and a long battle with rustlers. In the mid-1850s, Lewis, always renowned as a womanizer, was shot to death by the husband of his latest lover. King regrouped and brought in two other partners: his old riverboating partner Mifflin Kenedy, and James Walworth, who was a silent partner. It was also around this time that King married Henrietta Chamberlain, a pretty, cultured young woman, and the daughter of a Presbyterian minister. She was about 20 years younger than he was, but by all reports King was a handsome, youthful man, and certainly, in those days, a good catch. It seems to have been a solid marriage. The Kings had two daughters and a son. While the family was growing, the ranch also grew. By 1861 they had 20,000 head of cattle and 3,000 horses.

King had the foresight and intelligence to realize it would be to his advantage to improve his herd by careful breeding. He began importing British bulls and experimenting to raise better beef than the tough, stringy longhorns could produce. King also began raising and breeding horses, eventually producing what is now known as the Western Quarter Horse, a cross between the wild mustangs, pure-bred Spanish horses, and the English thoroughbred. The quarter horse was specifically bred to be a good cow horse. It needed to be very fast over short distances, rugged, nimble and intelligent. Today this breed of horse is one of the most common and popular in the United States.

During the Civil War, King's ranch did not prosper, but he made a fortune with his riverboat company by acting as a cotton agent for the Confederacy. After the war, King's biggest problem was dealing with the Mexican outlaw Juan Cortina, a Mexican aristocrat who was obsessed with exacting revenge from the Texans who had stolen his land. King estimated that Cortina rustled at least 50,000 head of his cattle, over a million dollars worth, within a few years after the war. After many gruesome deaths on both sides in what amounted to a minor war, the Texas Rangers were reassembled under Leander McNelly. In less than a year the Mexican bandits had been disbanded.

By the late 1870s, the King Ranch was worth many millions of dollars, and Richard King was known as the "King of Texas." He always operated his ranch conservatively, and yet was often the first to innovate and experiment. When King died in 1885, Henrietta continued to run the ranch, along with son-in-law Robert J. Kleberg, for 40 more years. During the time she was in charge of the King empire, she developed America's first breed of beef cattle, called the Santa Gertrudis. She practiced advanced feeding techniques and conservation of the land. She created an on-ranch program to preserve the wild game on the ranch, experimented with various species of grass, and implemented many other programs that were innovative, pro-

The aristocratic Juan Cortina (1824–1892) (*top*) was more than just a bandit. He saw himself as resisting gringo oppression, and led a revolt in Texas in 1859. Unfortunately, the Anglos didn't see it that way. Faced with the combined might of the U.S. Army and the Texas Rangers, Cortina fled to Mexico.

A panoramic view (*bottom*) of a Montana ranch, comfortable if not elegant, in 1872.

Granville Stuart (1834–1918) (*above left*) found gold in Montana in 1862, but never made much money from it. He settled in Deer Lodge in 1867 and became a storekeeper, pioneer rancher, community leader, and from 1894 to 1899, ambassador to Uruguay and Paraguay (appointed by President Cleveland). His vivid diaries are an important source for information about early Montana.

Awbonnie Tookanka Stuart (*above right*), Granville's wife of 26 years and mother of his five children.

A leading figure in Montana history in the second half of the eighteenth century was Samuel T. Hauser (1833–1914) (*facing top*). As a

ductive, and ultimately, profitable. When Henrietta died the ranch was incorporated, and has been run by descendants ever since. It is said to be the largest ranch in the world.

THE MONTANA BARONS

One of the most richly detailed and authentic histories of the settling of Montana can be found in the journals of Granville Stuart, a man who never became very wealthy, but who played a leading role in the growth of Montana.

Stuart first went West in his teens when his father joined the California Gold Rush. Granville and his brother James didn't have much luck in California, and in 1857 struck out for the East. Before they reached Salt Lake City, they were warned that the Mormons were in the midst of an uprising. Not wanting to get mixed up with angry Mormons and federal troops, the brothers headed north, led by an old mountain man named Joe Meek. With Joe they ended up spending the winter in a tent in a Montana valley, and fell in love with the country.

When spring arrived, the Stuart brothers decided to do some prospecting in Montana. They never struck it rich, but they did find some gold in the Deer Lodge valley. News of their find sparked a gold rush to Montana in 1862. Granville and James became road ranchers, buying stock cheaply from wagon trains that needed to

rancher, businessman, and banker, Hauser was involved in many projects for Montana development. He was also territorial governor from 1885 to 1887. This photo was taken in 1884.

Many an entrepreneur found that much more profit could be made by supplying the miners than by seeking gold himself. Conrad Kohrs (*facing middle*), who went on to run one of the largest cattle companies in the West, began by supplying fresh meat to hungry miners.

The first cattle herd to arrive in Montana was driven up the Texas Trail to the Yellowstone valley by Nelson Story (*facing bottom*) in 1866.

unload some of the burden. When they had built up a sizable herd of livestock they found a lush, green valley and built a cabin. They continued to prospect for gold and to raise and sell their livestock, and by the following spring both had taken Indian wives. Granville's Shoshoni wife, Awbonnie Tookanka, lived with him for 26 years and bore him five children.

Over the years Granville was a butcher, a blacksmith, and always, a writer and recorder of life in the frontier West. He died in 1918.

Meanwhile, a young man named Conrad Kohrs was making himself a wealthy man by supplying beef to the miners. He would buy cattle, butcher them, and sell the fresh meat. He built up his own herd at the same time. Kohrs married a woman from back East, Augusta Kruse, who at the age of 19 was apparently a bit shocked at the primitive living conditions. She kept her chin up, though, and eventually found herself at the helm of a large and prosperous ranch. The Kohrs Pioneer Cattle Company was known throughout the West as one of the largest and most successful.

Another character in Montana cattle history is Nelson Story, who started out driving freight wagons. When gold was discovered in Montana he turned to prospecting, and managed to collect $30,000 worth of gold. Seeing that there was a shortage of beef in Montana and a surplus of it in Texas, Story headed for Dallas with his small fortune and invested part of it in a herd of cattle. His long drive to Montana was one of the first, the longest, and most dangerous in the history of the cattle drives, because much of his route took him through hostile Indian territory. When he finally reached Montana, he sold most of his stock for ten times the price he had purchased it for, and took the best of the herd to start his own ranch. Within a decade he had become one of the leading cattle ranchers in the Northwest.

While his contemporaries became wealthy, Granville Stuart remained poor, and finally became a bookeeper in a bank whose president was an old friend named Samuel Hauser. A few years later Hauser talked him into going into the cattle business, forming a partnership with Andrew Jackson Davis and his brother Erwin Davis. The Davis-Hauser-Stuart partnership, known as the DHS Ranch, was a great success. Eventually the Davis share of the partnership was bought out by Conrad Kohrs.

It was during his tenure with the DHS Ranch, in the summer of 1884, that Granville Stuart became the leader of a Montana vigilante group determined to wipe out the rustlers and outlaws who plagued the area. He and the other ranchers knew that the huge outlaw gang known as "The Innocents" was secretly masterminded by a sheriff named Henry Plummer but they were never able to get him into a court of law. Eventually Stuart and 14 other men formed a civilian posse known as "The Stranglers," which ruthlessly sought out the Innocents and methodically hung them – Plummer was hung in 1864. Estimates of the number of people killed (women were also rounded up in this vengeful killing spree) range from 35 to 70.

A few years later, after the rustlers had been cleared out, the area was hit by a devastating drought followed by a very cold, long winter. The DHS herds were decimated and Stuart, sickened by the death of so many animals, got out of the ranching business. He dabbled in many other pursuits during his life, including four years as a U.S. diplomat in Uruguay and Paraguay.

THE LURE OF
SILVER AND GOLD

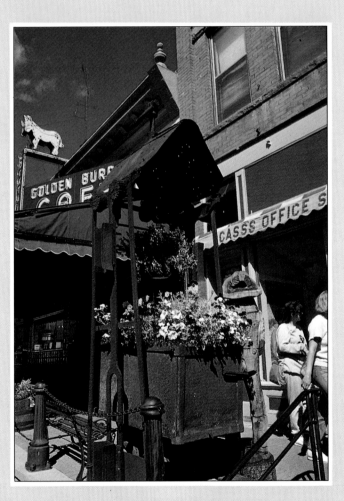

Colorado's mining heritage lives on today in the
restored areas of Leadville (elevation 10,188
feet). The city became the silver capital of the nation
in 1877. This old mining car is a relic of the boom
days from 1878 to 1881.

While thousands of hopeful Americans trudged westward to California after gold was discovered there in 1849, a few resourceful miners stopped in the Rockies to prospect there. Sure enough, gold was discovered, and the news spread quickly across the country. The first gold strike at Cherry Creek in 1859 turned the peaceful green valley, where Denver is now, into a tent city. A year later a very rich and seemingly endless vein of ore was struck at Clear Creek, attracting 15,000 people to Colorado in a matter of months, and over 50,000 in the next year.

The cry for the Colorado prospectors was "Pike's Peak or Bust!" The famous peak was usually the first landmark seen by the new settlers as they made their way across the vast prairies. Only a fraction of the thousands who started out for Colorado made it and stayed on. Those who did created small mining towns in the mountains, such as Aspen, Leadville, Central City, and Cripple Creek. One of the most flamboyant and sophisticated of the early mining towns was Helena, Montana. There were dozens of these small towns, most of them extremely rough and lawless. Only a handful remained after the gold and silver rush died down, leaving the Rockies a legacy of ghost towns.

THE BIRTH OF A MINING TOWN

Aspen was a good example of life in one of the more prosperous mining towns. The Ute Indians apparently thought there was something special about the valley of the "Thunder River" as they called the Roaring Fork, for they fought fiercely to keep it, giving up only after most of the tribe had been lost in a series of massacres. What inspired the first white settlers to move in was not the beauty of the valley, the abundance of game in the surrounding mountains, and the fish in the rivers, but the promise of rich silver veins.

The Western Slope of Colorado remained largely unexplored by miners for nearly a decade after the first ore strikes on the Front Range, because of the threat of Indians and the cost of setting up refineries and shipping the ore out. With the passage of the Sherman Silver Purchase Act in 1878, the federal treasury department bought silver each month and coined it into silver dollars. This type of guaranteed return on silver created a new wave of fortune-seekers willing to risk the Indians and the hard winters of the mountains.

When the first silver strike in the Roaring Fork Valley was made in 1879 near Independence Pass, where the ghost town of Independence still stands, Leadville was a well-established city. It became the supply center for Independence and Ute City, as Aspen was first named, even though access to the valley was far easier from the northwest, where Glenwood Springs is today. Even now the road over Independence Pass from Leadville is closed most of the year by snow, avalanches, and rock slides.

THE REIGN OF THE SILVER QUEEN

Henry Gillespie was an early supporter and promoter of Aspen. It was he who went to Washington to lobby for mail service, a telegraph line, and a road into town. B. Clark Wheeler had a reputation as a swindler and claim jumper, but he was also a smart, aggressive leader who ran the town in its first years, giving it a certain amount of

Historic Durango, Colorado (*top*), was a booming mining town in the 1860s. Some 50,000 people came to seek gold and silver in the great Pikes Peak rush of 1859.

Silverton, Colorado (*middle*), is perched high in the Rocky Mountains. Even today the road is often closed by winter weather.

The first important silver strike in Colorado was in Central City in 1859. By the mid-1860s, the surface ore was exhausted. In the 1870s and 1880s, improved extraction methods made Central City boom again, but by 1914 the silver was gone and the city was a ghost town. Today performances at the Central City Opera House draw visitors every summer, as does the annual Bed Race (*bottom*).

law and order. After staking out a good many claims for himself, he had the valley surveyed and laid out a townsite, changed the name from Ute City to Aspen, and then went on a lecture tour to draw settlers and investors to the Roaring Fork Valley.

Jerome B. Wheeler (no relation to Clark Wheeler), president of Macy's department store in New York, was lucky enough to be a partner in the Mollie Gibson, one of Aspen's richest mines. With the generosity and foresight that were to characterize his dealings with the fledgling town, he used the proceeds from the Mollie Gibson to build a smelter, a bank, an opera house, and a hotel. He was also involved in a marble quarry, coal and iron mines, and a ranch. Though both have recently been renovated on the inside, the Wheeler Opera House and the Hotel Jerome remain two of Aspen's handsomest and best-loved landmarks.

In 1889 Aspen had a population of 8,000, including eight doctors, 31 lawyers, and 500 mine owners. It had the best mining equipment available, three banks, 43 saloons, 23 hotels, 25 "sporting houses," ten churches, two schools, two railroads, three daily newspapers, and a county courthouse. Sturdy brick buildings which still stand today housed shops, and fanciful gingerbread Victorian homes lined the streets of the residential areas. Though the miners who frequented the red-light district on Durant Avenue led a typically rowdy lifestyle, Aspen maintained a sophistication and cultural élan that set it apart from other mining towns. A literary society and a temperance society were formed by the wives of mine owners even while they were still living in tents. Their husbands built polo grounds and a race track.

Central City in 1864 (*facing top*). The environmental destruction of mining is apparent in this photo – the hillsides are denuded of timber.

Prospectors endured poor conditions and hard labor in the hopes of striking it rich. This miner's cabin (*facing middle*) in the Sierra Nevada was photographed in 1866.

Gold fever: prospectors set off with an oxcart for the goldfields of the Black Hills in 1889 (*facing bottom*).

Main Street, Creede, Colorado, on June 1, 1892 (*above*). On June 5, the hastily constucted wooden buildings burned to the ground in a fire that swept the town.

Poverty Gulch in Cripple Creek, Colorado, in 1897 (*right*). Gold was discovered at Cripple Creek in 1890, making it the last but also the richest of the Colorado mining towns.

John Sutter (1803–1880) (*top right*) came to California from Switzerland in 1839. He received a large land grant near Sacramento and built a fort that became a profitable trading center for settlers. On January 24, 1849, a carpenter named James Marshall showed Sutter some rocks he had found in a stream bed. Sutter realized the ore was gold, and tried in vain to keep the find secret, but word leaked out and the great California gold rush was on.

Yreka, California (*top left*), was named by an optimistic but badly educated gold seeker in 1851. In the Klamath River region of northern California, Yreka was a virtual ghost town by the 1880s.

The Carson Valley on the eastern slope of the Sierra Nevada was the last resting place for gold hunters before beginning the final push into California. In 1850 a trading post called Mormon Station (*middle*) was established in the valley, incidentally becoming the first permanent settlement in the state of Nevada. The traders would buy exhausted animals cheaply from weary emigrants, feed the animals up and sell them again. Food prices were outrageously high, but the emigrants were in no position to bargain over paying $1.50 a pound for flour and $1 for a bunch of turnips.

Ironically, the gold on his land was John Sutter's destruction. His property (*bottom left*) was overrun with gold seekers. In 1852 Sutter moved to Washington, D.C., where he spent his time petitioning the government for compensation. The Supreme Court disallowed his claims.

Many went to California to make their fortune, but most found hardship and poverty instead. This caricature of a California gold miner (*bottom right*) appeared in 1853.

D.R.C. Brown, father of one of the founders of the Aspen Skiing Corporation, started an electric company, making Aspen the first town in Colorado with electric street lights. These were the heady days when the miners worked shifts round the clock. Winter and summer, they could be seen making their way up and down Aspen Mountain, then known as Ajax. At night they carried torches, and it was this sight that later inspired Aspen's tradition of skiing down Ajax in torchlight parades.

In 1893 the U.S. government suddenly repealed the Sherman Act and demonetized silver. At that time Aspen was the largest silver camp in the world and the busiest town between Denver and Salt Lake City. But its economic well-being was based on silver, and the repeal of the Sherman Act spelled disaster. Almost overnight the mines shut down, banks closed their doors, businesses folded, and the population dropped to 1,000. By 1930 Aspen was virtually a ghost town, with a population of less than 600 and street after street of empty houses.

Most mining towns were not pleasant places to live unless mine owners who struck it rich poured substantial amounts of money into them. Boulder, Colorado was described as a "God-forsaken little hole," and another town was called a "sewer five miles long." The mines and their tailings made (and still make) unsightly scars on the mountains. Tailing dumps surrounded many of the towns, trees were generally stripped from the mountains to be used as timber in the mines, and, because of the lack of government structure, sanitation was non existent.

The get-rich-quick lure of the gold and silver rush in the Rockies attracted men and women who tended to be gamblers and dreamers. The miners themselves were hard workers – some of them hoping to get in on the riches, some of them just trying to make a decent living. Many of the miners emigrated to the United States from the exhausted mines of Cornwall in southwest England and from the mountains of Italy.

The hand-painted ceiling of the Central City Opera House (*top left*) was created by artist John Massmann in 1878. It is one of the largest muraled ceilings in the country.

Piper's Opera House in Virginia City (*top right*) is the oldest working theater in the West. Great performers such as Enrico Caruso, Harry Houdini, Al Jolson, Mark Twain, and John Philip Sousa appeared here.

So much silver was mined in Colorado that the United States Bureau of the Mint opened a branch office (*bottom*) there in 1897.

A saloon interior in Telluride, Colorado, around 1875.

Some of the prospectors fell in love with the grandeur and beauty of the Rockies and stayed on, making a living off the land. One of these was a man named Joel Estes, who fell in love with the valley now named Estes Park just outside of Rocky Mountain National Park in Colorado. In 1867 he and his son Milton described the streams overflowing with trout, the plentiful grass, and the abundance of game. They built a cabin, sent for the rest of the family, and settled in.

Following hot upon the heels of any gold or silver strike and subsequent mining town, no matter how rough, were those who could be seen either as providing services to the miners or as taking full advantage of the miners. These were the people who operated the saloons, the brothels, the gambling houses, and the hotels.

UNCLE DICK WOOTTON

One of the most famous of these characters was Richens Lacy Wootton, a Virginian who headed West in 1836 at the age of twenty and became a trapper, exploring the Rockies with men like Kit Carson. When the trapping era came to an end, Wootton became a

Virginia City, Nevada, (*above*) from a nearby hillside in 1868. Within a few weeks of the discovery of gold here in 1863, 10,000 miners were camped in the area.

Blonde and beautiful Elizabeth McCourt Doe Tabor, better known as Baby Doe, in an undated photo (*below*) taken probably around 1885.

J. C.H. Grabill's mining exchange (*right*) in Colorado, 1888. The lively – and often dishonest – trade in mining shares made and lost fortunes. Grabill, who took this picture, was also a photographer; his studio is at left.

classic frontier scout, Indian fighter, and entrepreneur. One of his schemes included raising tame buffalo to sell to zoos and circuses. He drove nine thousand sheep to California to sell to gold rush settlers and came back with a herd of Spanish mules, which he sold for a tidy profit. He opened a blacksmith shop, and ran a wagon train that hauled freight from Missouri to New Mexico.

When the Pikes Peak gold rush began, Wootton, who was now called "Uncle Dick" Wootton, quickly made an appearance with a load of "Taos Lightning" whiskey, causing much joy and celebration in the new town of Denver. He subsequently opened a saloon and a hotel in Denver.

Uncle Dick Wootton was a Confederate sympathizer, and when the Civil War broke out he moved south to Pueblo. Ever restless, he then built a badly needed road over Raton Pass into New Mexico, opening it in 1866. He also built an inn, and charged everyone but the Indians a toll to use the road. When the Atchison, Topeka and Santa Fe Railroad wanted the right-of-way over the pass, Uncle Dick sold it to them in 1879 for a lifelong pension and retired. He lived, growing more legendary every year, until 1893.

James Joseph Brown (*left*) made his fortune in mining. He met his wife, Molly, in Leadville; they were married in 1886. In 1894 they moved to Denver, purchased a home, and became prominent in Denver society. Molly survived the sinking of the *Titanic*, thus earning the nickname "the Unsinkable Molly Brown." The Molly Brown House is preserved today as a memorial.

Horace Tabor built a lavish opera house (*right*) for Leadville from the profits of his Little Pittsburg mine. It stands today.

H. A. W. TABOR

Many a grocery- and supply-store owner made it rich by supplying prospectors with food and supplies (called a grub stake) in exchange for a stake in a mine. The most famous of these merchants was a flamboyant and tragic man named Horace Austin Warner Tabor. Tabor was born in Vermont in 1830 and became a stonecutter. He had always had political ambitions, and went to Kansas in 1855, where he was elected to the legislature. Two years later he returned to New England and married Augusta Pierce. Soon after his marriage, Tabor got wind of the Pikes Peak gold rush, and set out for Colorado with his wife and infant son Maxcy, arriving in 1859.

For fifteen years the Tabors moved around the Colorado gold and silver fields. Most often, Horace was the town postmaster, and Augusta ran a boarding house. Horace dreamed of great riches, while Augusta just hoped for a pump outside her front door so she didn't have to haul water up from the creek. In 1860 they opened a store in Oro City, a small town near Leadville. This town was so remote that when Augusta arrived, the miners were so glad to see a woman that they rejoiced and built her a cabin.

When the news of a rich strike at Leadville came, the Tabors once again moved, this time to a town called Buckskin Joe, where they lived for seven years.

Tabor had made it a practice to grubstake prospectors, so when in the late 1870s two German shoemakers came into his store asking for food, he gave them $17's worth for a third interest in their mine, and sent them on their way. The story goes that the shoemakers got into Tabor's liquor. They were so drunk that a few miles out of town they sat down under a tree, and in their stupor began digging under it. Three feet under they hit a rich silver vein that became the Little Pittsburg mine and brought H. A. W. Tabor $500,000.

The interior of Piper's Opera House today is much as it was more than a hundred years ago.

Out of that one grub stake, Tabor became a millionaire many times over. He became the mayor of Leadville, and served as lieutenant governor of Colorado from 1879 to 1883. He built Leadville an opulent opera house which still stands. In Denver he built an opera house and the Tabor Block, Denver's first tall building. Tabor's wealth and extravagance became a worldwide legend. Meanwile, Augusta, who had run a boarding house for so many years, had concerns about Tabor's reckless spending. Tabor found himself a beautiful young, blonde, blue-eyed divorcee named Elizabeth McCourt Doe, who was known as Baby Doe. Eventually he divorced Augusta and married Baby Doe, who thoroughly enjoyed spending his millions.

Unfortunately, Augusta's words of warning would have been well heeded. In the 1880s Tabor made bad investments in paper railroads and worthless South African mines. When the Sherman Silver Purchase Act was repealed in 1893 Tabor's mines died, leaving him not just penniless, but heavily in debt. His friends used political connections to get Tabor a position as postmaster of Denver in 1898, a

The simplest way to find gold is to pan for it. This is an effective technique if the gold lies in deposits near the surface where running water will wash it into the stream bed. This photo (*top left*) was taken near Virginia City, Montana Territory, in 1871.

Cradling for gold with a rocker is an improvement over panning. Gold-bearing soil is shoveled into the cradle or rocker, where the soil is washed away by the stream, leaving the heavier gold behind. This photo (*top right*) was taken near Virginia City in 1871.

Hydraulic mining (*middle left*) took the simple concept of panning for gold to its ultimate form. Water was piped under pressure over stream banks and hillsides. The soil and gravel was washed through sluice boxes, leaving behind the ore. The environmental destruction this caused was enormous.

Cars come out of the shaft in the Comstock Mine around 1868 (*middle right*).

Once the ore was removed from the mine, it needed to be processed to remove the precious metals. Ox carts haul the ore to the Montezuma silver smelting works in Orena, Nevada in 1868 in this photo (*bottom left*).

"Clean up" day at the Deadwood gold stamping mill, 1888 (*bottom right*). The ore was crushed by steam-powered stamps as if in a huge mortar and pestle.

Lode mining, when the ore is underground, is more complex and dangerous. Here (*top left*) a miner works in the Comstock Mine in Virginia City, Nevada Territory in 1868.

Horses pulled ore carts along rails laid in the mine. When the tunnels were too small for horses, human musclepower pulled the carts instead. This photo (*top right*) was taken in the Bobtail Mine in Black Hawk Canyon, Colorado, in 1898.

Placer mining with a rocker in Tuolumne County, California, in 1866 (*middle left*).

A big strike brought miners running. Here (*middle right*) miners with picks, sledgehammers, and shovels pose on a rocky hill at the newly discovered Racine Boy Mine in Silver Cliff, Colorado, in 1880.

A closer view of the smelting works in Orena, taken in 1873 (*bottom left*). Note the silver bars neatly stacked in the center.

Part of the great Homestake Mine complex in Lead City, Dakota Territory, in 1889 (*bottom right*). The huge slag pile in the foreground is an indication of the scale of the works.

Chief Ouray (the Arrow), a Southern Ute. Alfred Packer's party refused to listen to his advice about the winter weather of the Rockies. All except Alfred ended up eaten.

position he held until his death a year later. On his deathbed, Tabor instructed Baby Doe to "hold onto the Matchless," one of his favorite mines, which he had managed to keep. She followed his instructions and moved up to Leadville, where she lived in a shack next to the Matchless. The remaining 35 years of her life were spent in extreme poverty, and when she died in 1935 the Leadville paper reported that she had frozen to death. The romance and tragedy of Horace, Augusta, and Baby Doe Tabor is the theme of the opera *The Ballad of Baby Doe.* Appropriately, this work by Douglas Moore had its world premiere in the Central City opera house in 1956.

By 1880 Leadville had five banks, three newspapers, seven churches, and seven schools, of which this is one. The city also had 120 saloons, 118 gambling houses, and 35 brothels.

THE COLORADO CANNIBAL

Every year students at the University of Colorado have what they call "Alfred Packer Memorial Day," an orgy of food, feasting, eating, and cooking contests. The subject of this high-spirited memorial is a mountain guide who led a party of men from Utah to Colorado in the mining days. Before tackling the San Juan mountains of southern Colorado they camped on the Uncompahgre River near the Los Pinos Indian Agency, which was the camp of the Ute Chief Ouray. Winter was setting in with a vengeance, and Ouray advised the twenty men to spend the winter there. Half the party stayed at Los Pinos, and the other half, led by Alfred Packer, pushed on.

Many weeks later Packer appeared alone at Los Pinos, with the story that the other men had abandoned him when he was unable to keep up because of snow blindness. However, Ouray and others became suspicious when they noticed that Packer did not show signs of hardship, had an unusually large amount of money, and carried the belongings of some of the other men. Eventually he admitted that they had been stranded in a blizzard with no food. According to Packer, after one member of the party who was 60 years old died of starvation, his companions had eaten him. Within a few weeks the only person alive was Packer, who had survived by eating his companions, one by one. Packer was tried for his crime and got 40 years of hard labor.

ARMY LIFE, ARMY HEROES

This portrait of courageous, dashing, long-haired
General George Armstrong Custer is so familiar
as to be an icon of the Indian wars.

President James Polk (*top*) ordered U.S. troops to the Rio Grande in 1846, starting the Mexican-American War.

John Coffee Hays (*bottom*) led the regiment of Texas Rangers that fought with Zachary Taylor and Winfield Scott in the Mexican-American War.

Zachary Taylor (*facing left*) was sent to Corpus Christi, Texas with 1,500 men in July of 1845. In the spring of 1846 he moved his troops into disputed territory; on April 25 he was attacked by Mexican troops. Taylor became a national hero during the war that followed. He was elected president in 1848.

Military expeditions for the purpose of exploration, and small outposts or forts in the wilderness of the American West, were the extent of the military presence on the frontier for many years. It was the Mexican-American war in 1848 that first galvanized an American president into sending in the troops to do battle.

The opening of the Santa Fe Trail into New Mexico created a steady stream of merchants, soon followed by settlers. The settlers staked out claims on land rightfully owned by Mexicans and Indians, so naturally, tensions in the area were high. In 1846, President Polk dispatched General Stephen Watts Kearney to do battle with the Mexicans. The U.S. Army was joined by the Texas Rangers, who became famous for their exploits. However, in reality there was very little resistance from the Mexicans, and the so-called war resembled an occupation more than a battle. Just two years after Kearney went to the Southwest, the United States signed a treaty with Mexico, paying $15 million for a huge area of land encompassing present-day New Mexico, Arizona, Utah, Nevada, California, and part of Colorado.

THE TEXAS RANGERS

The Texas Rangers were formed in the 1840s to protect white settlers from raids by Indians and Mexicans. They began their careers with a reputation as a gang of lazy, worthless vigilantes. However, a Captain Tumlinson and a private Noah Smithwick became famous for hunting down and rescuing a small boy from marauding Apaches, and returning him safely to his mother. After that episode the Texas Rangers were known as heroes who, like the Canadian Mounties, always "got their man."

The Rangers were primarily fighting two other cultural groups whose land the Americans had occupied without permission – the Indians and the Mexicans. Naturally, the Rangers became known for their ability to "ride like a Mexican, trail like an Indian, shoot like a Tennessean, and fight like the devil." Their code of ethics said that they must always be prepared to offer their life for the life of a fellow Ranger, and that they must never surrender to the enemy.

Captain John Coffee Hays was the best-known of the Texas Rangers. He went to Texas when he was 25 years old, looking for a good fight. He was soon made a captain, and his first major victory was in defending San Antonio from a group of Mexicans who didn't agree that Texas was now part of the United States. He was badly outnumbered, and managed to trick the Mexicans into retreating. Hays also became known for his skill in fighting Indians.

Another Texas Ranger who won the hearts of many was a gentle, courageous giant of a man known as Big Foot Wallace. He was a hero of the settlers whose lives he protected, and was known as a great story teller. When there was no longer any need to protect whites from attacks by Mexicans and Indians, Big Foot Wallace took a job driving a stagecoach from Austin to El Paso.

After the Civil War, the Texas Rangers were reorganized to help bring the law to the wild Texas frontier. In the period between 1874 and 1890 the Rangers enforced the law with great success, helping rid Texas of numerous cattle thieves, bandits, Indian raiders, and killers. Today 62 Texas Rangers, each trained in the most advanced criminal investigation techniques, continue a long tradition of law enforcement.

THE WEST AFTER THE CIVIL WAR

During the Civil War there was relatively little military presence in the West, and as a result the Southwest was nearly lost to the Confederates. After the Civil War, the army decommissioned many men, and reduced the rank of many officers. As a result, competition and jealousy among officers over promotions was intense. Much of that tension was taken out in fighting Indians – the way to a promotion was to win battles with the Indians.

For an enlisted man, a stint in the post-Civil War U.S. Army of the West during the Indian Wars was about as tough a life as a man could choose. Discipline was heavy-handed and probably largely random – whoever got caught in a breach of conduct was severely punished. Even the smallest infraction, such as sleeping through roll call, legally required a court martial.

There were literally thousands of court martials. The lesser breaches of conduct might draw a punishment of a day's forced march under a heavy load, or being strung up by the wrists or

Desertion was a serious problem among troops stationed in the West. The punishment for those caught was death – here (*top*) a soldier of the 8th Infantry is executed at Prescott, Arizona, in 1877. In practice, however, the death penalty was not often given, and most deserters were never caught.

Soldiers of the 6th Cavalry break horses at Fort Bayard, New Mexico, in 1885 (*middle*).

Troop C of the 5th Cavalry around 1888 (*bottom*).

A company of the 16th Infantry camps near Fort Davis, Texas, around 1887 (top).

In this reenactment, (bottom) General Stephen Watts Kearney arrives with his cavalry at Bent's Old Fort in Colorado. The actual event happened in 1846, at the start of the Mexican-American War.

thumbs. Harsher punishment might have included being fined a month's pay and given a month in prison, or both. Deserters wore a ball and chain around the ankle for as many months as their superiors deemed necessary. For insubordination and a dozen other crimes, soldiers could be executed.

About a third of all those recruited during the Indian Wars deserted, and it's no wonder. Most of them had little or no training, and were poorly equipped to fight the Indians. It was a thankless job, with low pay, dangerous and uncomfortable living conditions, and poor food. Few enlisted men saved their meager wages, because they were usually in debt to officers and storekeepers.

The U.S. Army of the West was an all-volunteer group signed up for three- to five-year hitches. They were typical of the American melting pot, being a mixture of many cultures and ethnic groups, and from all walks of society. Many were lured by the glamour of the wild, wild West, and ended up sadly disillusioned.

In post-Civil War America, the black regiments were segregated off by themselves. Though they got little credit for it, they had a

After the Civil War two infantry regiments – the 24th and 25th – and two cavalry regiments – the 9th and 10th – were made up of black soldiers serving under white officers. One of the most famous officers was Colonel Benjamin Henry Grierson (1826–1911) (*top left*). Under his command the 10th Cavalry had a fine record in combat against the Indians. At a time when many officers refused to command black soldiers, and when many officers were confirmed Indian-haters, Grierson was known for his humane interest in both.

The band of the 9th Cavalry (*top right*) plays for the Fourth of July on the plaza at Santa Fe, New Mexico, in 1880.

Blacks were also assigned as servants to white officers. Here (*middle*) two soldiers assist an officer's wife and her children at a camp in central Arizona in the late 1880s.

In this drawing from 1888 (*bottom right*) by Frederic Remington, a black cavalry trooper takes a pull at his canteen. Black soldiers were nicknamed buffalo soldiers by the Indians, in reference to their curly hair.

Black soldiers were often assigned to undesirable duties. Here they guard a typical stagewagon (*bottom left*) of the Concord type around 1869.

John Charles Frémont (1813–1890) (*top*) explored many areas of the West in the course of several important expeditions in the 1840s. In 1856 he was nominated for president by the newly formed Republican Party, but lost to James Buchanan.

Frémont became a popular American hero. In this somewhat fanciful woodcut from the 1840s (*middle*), he is shown planting the American standard on the Rocky Mountains.

The writings of Frémont's wife, Jessie Benton Frémont (daughter of the powerful Senator from Missouri, Thomas Hart Benton) (*bottom*), helped foster the legend of Frémont the great explorer after the Civil War, when his reputation was tarnished by military and business failure.

reputation for smart, disciplined, and courageous fighting. The Indians had a healthy respect for the black regiments, calling them the "Buffalo Soldiers," supposedly a comparison between the curly coats of the buffalo and the hair of the black soldiers.

With a few exceptions, the so-called heroes who made a name for themselves in the U.S. military fighting Indians and Mexicans were not particularly admirable men. In fact, most of them won their renown for the ruthless and cold-blooded slaughter of Indians.

JOHN CHARLES FRÉMONT

One of the earliest military trailblazers was John C. Frémont, a topographer and promoter par excellence, who made five expeditions to the West between 1842 and 1854, becoming known to the public as "The Pathfinder." In reality he found very few paths, and most of his expeditions were disastrous because of poor judgment on his part. For all his rash decisions, Frémont was a romantic figure. He had enormous energy and enthusiasm, intelligence, good looks, and lots of connections. He was known as a social climber. His father-in-law was Senator Thomas Hart Benton, one of the most vocal and powerful proponents of Manifest Destiny and the expansion of the United States of America all the way to the Pacific Ocean.

Frémont's expeditions did produce semi-accurate maps of much of the American West. More important, his vivid and highly romanticized accounts of his journeys, written with his brilliant wife Jessie Benton Frémont, stirred up a great migration fever among Americans. His maps also served the purpose of giving American leaders a route for sending fighting troops into California – should that be necessary.

Frémont's first expedition to the West in 1842 was led by Kit Carson (who Frémont made a hero in his writings). They mapped South Pass, a route through the mountains discovered by trapper Jedediah Smith. From there they went to the Wind River Range, where Frémont picked a mountain, named it the tallest in the Rockies, and proceeded to try to climb it. According to his hard-working German topographer Charles Preuss, Frémont never did make it to the top, but his thrilling account of planting the stars and stripes on top of the highest peak probably lured thousands of young dreamers West.

Frémont remained a heroic, colorful, and somewhat reckless character for most of his life. He led the famous Bear Flag Rebellion against Mexico in California in 1846, was a California senator in 1850, and a Republican candidate for president in 1856, losing to James Buchanan. He became an unsuccessful if not incompetent Union general in the Civil War, and later served as governor of the Arizona territory from 1878 to 1881. He died, poor and obscure, in 1890.

GENERAL SHERIDAN AND GENERAL SHERMAN

During the 1870s the military command of Lieutenant General Philip Henry Sheridan was the Division of the Missouri, an area that encompassed the Dakotas, the northern and southern plains, and the Rocky Mountains. These also happened to be the areas where, at that time, the Indian Wars were being fought most fiercely by the Sioux, the Cheyenne, the Kiowas, and the Comanches. The Department of the Missouri had become famous during the Civil War under the command of Lieutenant General William Tecumseh Sherman. When Sherman was made commander of the entire U.S. Army, Sheridan was promoted to his position with the Division of the Missouri.

Sheridan had his hands full with his command. The U.S. government was doing everything in its power to induce people to settle in the West, and Sheridan had the task of trying to protect these settlers from the righteously indignant Indians whose lands were being taken from them.

Sherman wasn't much help. He so hated Washington and its politics that he moved his military headquarters to St. Louis, preferring what he perceived as the freedom, simplicity, and directness of the West and its people. Sherman was a man obsessed by his mission to settle the West and exterminate the Indians in the process. He had no patience for negotiation or diplomacy. To Sherman, sheer, brute force was the way to accomplish things.

Sherman was often off somewhere in the wilds of the West, fighting small battles, and Sheridan's patience was often tested trying to co-operate with the moody Sherman. President Ulysses Grant was an admirer of Sheridan, saying, "I believe General Sheridan has no superior as a general either living or dead, and perhaps not an equal." Sheridan was reportedly one of those generals who was admired and respected by his men because he did not ask them to endure any hardship that he would not endure himself. At the same time, he was not one to cut his men any slack, and had a low tolerance for stupid or foolish behavior.

Sheridan had a weakness for the good life, and as he grew older his already oddly square, squat body became very round. He had a reputation as a man who enjoyed good food, good drink, and dancing with beautiful women.

Sheridan's directive was to conquer the Plains Indians, which eventually he did in the campaign against the southern tribes in 1874–75 and against the Sioux in 1876–77. His tactics included much treachery and the killing of women and children as a means of extermination.

Although Lieutenant General Philip Henry Sheridan (seated at center) (*top*) is often accused of saying, "The only good Indians I ever saw were dead," it is by no means clear that the sentiment originated with him.

General Sherman and Bureau of Indian Affairs commissioners in council with Indian chiefs at Fort Laramie, Wyoming, in 1867 or 1868 (*middle*).

General William Tecumseh Sherman (1820–1891) (*bottom*) believed the Indians should be forced onto reservations and made to remain there. During his command of the Division of the Missouri from 1866 to 1869, he put this belief into action against the Plains Indians.

MAJOR GEORGE A. FORSYTH

Major George Forsyth was famous as an Indian fighter. He had fought with General Sheridan in the Civil War and was respected for his aggressiveness and resourcefulness – traits belied by his boyish good looks. Forsyth was born in 1837. He entered the army as a private at the start of the Civil War; he retired with the rank of brevet brigadier general. When in 1868 General Sheridan realized that traditional military techniques would not win against the guerilla warfare of the Sioux and Cheyenne Indians, he took Forsyth's suggestion to hand-pick a group of 50 men to fight them.

Forsyth was best known for the Battle of Beecher's Island in 1868. He and his band of men followed an Indian trail to a huge encampment of Sioux and Cheyenne in eastern Colorado. Forsyth's men made camp, not knowing that the Indians had spotted them. The next morning they awoke to find themselves surrounded by some 750 painted Indians, ready for a fight. Forsyth rounded up his men on an island in the middle of a river, where they dug in and fought off the Indians for six days, until reinforcements rescued them.

Powell reported on the spectacular scenery of the Grand Canyon (*above*) in his classic *Exploration of the Colorado River*, published in 1875. Much of the book is based on his journals of the 1869 expedition.

Powell and his men were the first to see much of the Colorado River and the astonishing canyons that it forms. This (*top right*) is Marble Canyon in Arizona.

In 1871 Powell led a second expedition down the Colorado River. This photo (*bottom right*) shows the first camp in the willows of the Green River, Wyoming Territory.

In 1869, John Wesley Powell (1834–1902) (*far right*), a Civil War hero who had lost an arm at Shiloh, led an expedition of ten men in four small boats down the rapids-filled Colorado and Green rivers. They passed through the entire length of the Grand Canyon and emerged three months later as national heroes.

Fort Bowie, Arizona, was strategically located by a spring on the east side of Apache Pass. It was a base of operations for General Crook and General Miles in their campaigns against Geronimo and his band of Apaches. When they were finally captured, the group was kept prisoner here before being sent to exile in Florida. Just the ruins, accessible today only by footpath, remain.

Though the battle of Beecher's Island (named after second-in-command Lieutenant Frederick Beecher, who died in the battle) didn't have much effect either way in the Indian wars, it became a symbol for the rest of the U.S. Army of the bravery and resourcefulness of the enlisted man.

GENERAL GEORGE CROOK

General George Crook was an Indian fighter best known for his role in the events leading to the battle of Little Big Horn. In 1876, as part of a three-pronged attack, he was to approach a huge encampment of Indians from the south. He and his force of about 1,200 men were turned back by at least 1,000 Indians at the Rosebud River. This kept him from uniting his forces with those of General Alfred Terry, and enabled the Sioux and Cheyenne warriors to join up with others on the Little Big Horn River, where they later met and destroyed Custer and his men.

Crook is less known for the fact that he was an eccentric but humane and intelligent leader. In an era when military promotions were scarce and jealously fought over, Crook went from the rank of lieutenant colonel to brigadier general in one fell swoop. He earned his promotion in 1871 by being willing and able to lead the Division of Arizona in a harsh, unsettled area where settlers were terrorized by roving bands of fierce Apache Indians.

Alkali Lake in the Carson Desert, Nevada, with expedition members standing on the shores (*top*). Timothy O'Sullivan took this photo in 1873.

Fred Loring, in his campaign costume, with his mule Evil Merodach, in 1871 (*middle left*). Loring worked with Wheeler as general assistant and correspondent. He was killed by Indians.

Frontiersman P. Cook (*middle right*) with his rifle and mule. Cook was one of many local guides hired by Wheeler in the course of his surveys.

Photographer Timothy O'Sullivan, who was famous for his Civil War photos, accompanied Wheeler on many of his travels. The photographic record he compiled was the first systematic look at many Western locations. This view (*bottom*) shows a camp on the Black Canyon of the Colorado River in 1874.

The Green River Canyon, Colorado (*top left*), taken from the top of the canyon wall by Timothy O'Sullivan in 1874.

Mount Agassiz, Utah, in a photo by Timothy O'Sullivan (*top right*).

Between 1871 and 1879, when the United States Geological Survey was created, the United States Army organized a number of surveys that mapped most of Arizona, New Mexico, Nevada, Colorado, and California. George M. Wheeler (1842–1905) led several of these expeditions. Here (*bottom left*) an expedition starts from Camp Mohave, Arizona, in 1871.

A member of the Wheeler Expedition sketches the ancient ruins in the Canyon de Chelly, Arizona, in 1873 (*bottom right*).

Crook was one of the few military men who saw the Indians as human beings being forcefully displaced from their land. He was fair and honest in his dealings with them. After defeating the Apaches in a series of battles, he immediately turned his attention toward assisting them in leading peaceful lives. This meant that the members of this nomadic warrior tribe had to learn to be farmers, ranchers, and shepherds. He taught them how to use irrigation ditches, and he taught them the American concept of buying and selling marketable items such as wool.

This unusual general also loved publicity, and often had a cadre of journalists accompanying him. In one photograph he is wearing an ostrich feather on his hat. He was known for riding into battle perched on a mule, dressed in a pith helmet and white canvas suit. He braided his long beard so that it appeared forked, and whittled on wood incessantly. Crook was also one of those rare Western heroes who didn't drink, smoke, or curse.

Crook was considered eccentric for his wide use of army mules, but this was a resourceful move that accounted for much of his success in fighting the Indians. He devised a special pack for them which allowed the animals to carry twice their normal load and move

General George Crook genuinely cared about the fate of the Indians. Knowing that the Apache's old way of life was doomed, he helped them adapt to the new ways. This Apache rancheria (*above*) was photographed some time in the 1880s.

A council between General Crook and Geronimo, 1886 (*below*). Geronimo is just to the left of the center, wearing a scarf on his head; General Crook is at right, wearing gloves.

quickly at the same time. They were much more able to endure hardships, such as lack of water and lack of good pasture, than horses, and he found they became excellent and reliable mounts when treated properly.

General Crook died in March of 1890, before the shameful battle of Wounded Knee of that year, in which many Sioux were massacred. Chief Red Cloud said of him, "He never lied to us. His words gave the people hope."

LIEUTENANT COLONEL GEORGE ARMSTRONG CUSTER

George Armstrong Custer said, early on in his military career, that he wanted to become famous. There's some question as to whether Custer is famous or infamous, but he clearly has a place secured in the annals of American history for his role in the disastrous Battle of Little Big Horn.

The son of a blacksmith in Ohio, Custer somehow managed to get himself into West Point, and then graduated last in his class. In spite of his class position at West Point, Custer quickly made a name for himself during the Civil War for a series of aggressive, reckless, and successful cavalry attacks that gained important ground for the Union.

It's not entirely clear how Custer climbed so quickly in rank, but by the time he was 23 years old he had been made a brevet brigadier

The blockhouse of Fort Abraham Lincoln (*above*). Custer and his 7th Cavalry were stationed here in 1873. On May 17, 1876, they rode out to meet their fates at the Little Bighorn River.

Cinching and loading a pack mule with flour barrels during General Crook's expedition to the Black Hills, 1876 (*below*).

The sun dance (*top*) is the central religious ceremony of the Plains Indian culture. Usually held in June or July, the ritual did not involve sun worship. Rather, the dance was an annual expression of tribal unity. The self-torture sometimes practiced by participants was intended to show individual sacrifice for the good of the tribe – the central ethic of the Plains Indians. This sun dance was held in New Mexico in 1888.

George Armstrong Custer (*left*) dressed in a buckskin hunting outfit, 1872.

A hunting and camping party (*above*) hosted by Custer (standing in center) at Fort Abraham Lincoln on the Little Heart River, Dakota Territory, 1875.

general of volunteers. The press quickly picked up on the story of the "boy general," who made quite a dramatic picture with his six-foot frame, broad shoulders, long, curly blond hair, and bright blue eyes. He designed his own flamboyant uniform, and wore a large sword, a trophy he bragged about taking from a Confederate officer he had shot in the back. At the end of the war Custer was the Army's youngest major general. He had that kind of boundless, restless energy that so many heroes of the American West seemed to possess, and was extremely ambitious.

Custer was also a favorite of General Philip Sheridan, who must have been instrumental in securing him a position as a lieutenant colonel in the Seventh Cavalry, which was formed in Kansas in 1867.

By all accounts, George Armstrong Custer had a very big ego and a strong craving for fame and fortune. He was keenly aware, as were so many other U.S. Army officers of the time, that the more Indians he conquered the better his chances of rising in the ranks. The few chances Custer did get to fight Indians were not tragedies, but they certainly were not victories. His reputation for poor judgment grew, but his reputation for fearless, blind, rushing attacks overshadowed the fact that he had no skill as a tactician.

Custer twice almost ruined his chances for military fame. Once he was court-martialed for desertion after leaving his company to visit his wife, Elizabeth Bacon. He was suspended without rank or pay for a year, but ended up being reinstated after ten months. Later he traveled to Washington and testified against President Grant, implicating the nation's leader and his relatives in a scandal. Grant ordered Custer out of the West, but pleas from General Alfred Terry once again got him reinstated.

The Battle of Little Big Horn in 1876 had its origins in the desire of the military to round up the Sioux and Cheyenne Indians and force them onto reservations. The Army knew that in June thousands upon thousands of Indians would gather along the banks of the Little Big Horn River for their annual Sun Dance – the biggest celebration of the year. The plan was to launch a three-pronged attack on the encampment. Two of the three prongs – those led by General Crook and General Terry – ran into trouble almost immediately, and pulled

The only survivor of the Battle of Little Bighorn was Custer's horse Comanche, photographed at the battlefield on June 27, 1876 (*top left*).

Dull Knife, chief of the Northern Cheyennes (*top right*) at Little Bighorn, in an undated photograph.

The scene of Custer's last stand, looking in the direction of the Indian village (*above*). A pile of bones remains on the Little Bighorn battlefield in 1877.

Some 268 soldiers died with Custer. They are buried at the battlefield, which is now a national monument (*top*).

back. Custer was part of the third prong, and he insisted on pushing ahead with a small force of men. He was ordered, in writing, to limit his movements to a reconnoitering of the Indians, but in his greed for dead Indian bodies he attacked. His 225 men were slaughtered by thousands of Indians. The only survivor on the white side in the Battle of Little Big Horn was an officer's horse named Comanche.

According to an account of the battle by the Sioux Chief Sitting Bull, Custer was among the last to die, surrounded by his fallen men, holding an empty pistol in his hand. Custer was among the few white men who was left with his scalp on, reportedly a sign of respect on the part of the Indians for the man they called "Long Hair."

The Indian wars were finally settled at a council of Sioux chiefs and leaders held at Pine Ridge, South Dakota, in 1891 (*bottom*).

COMMUNICATION AND TRANSPORTATION

The Conestoga wagon was developed by Pennsylvania Dutch craftsmen of the Conestoga River valley in the late 1700s. The back wheels were larger than the front ones, and the iron-shod tires were designed for dirt roads. The Conestoga was meant to haul goods, not passengers, so the driver usually walked beside. They were traditionally painted in the colors shown here. Wagons following this general design were used extensively by emigrants to the West, but not all were true Conestogas.

Covered wagons (*top*) preparing to head West crowd a street in Lawrence, Kansas, in the 1860s.

In 1849 John Butterfield (1801–1869) (*above*) organized the Butterfield and Watson Express Company. He soon joined with Wells and Company and Livingston, Fargo and Company to form the American Express Company – a firm that thrives today in much altered form.

It was in the late 1840s, four decades after Lewis and Clark made their overland journey to the Pacific Ocean, before substantial numbers of people began migrating to California. The settlers in those first wagon trains were motivated by the promise of rich gold strikes in California. There were daily risks to life and limb, ranging from rattlers and poisonous waterholes, to Indian attacks and the mountainous terrain of two high ranges, the Rockies and the Sierras.

Those heading for California had only that area on their minds. Denver, Colorado remained a green, quiet valley for another decade until "Pikes Peak or Bust" became the slogan of those heading for the gold of Clear Creek.

There was no overland mail service between the east and west coasts until the 1850s. What mail service there was went from New York City, via steamers, to the isthmus of Panama. From there passengers and letters were loaded into canoes and onto mules for the trip across the narrow strip of land to the Pacific Ocean, where another fleet of ocean steamers waited to take them to San Francisco. In 1855 a railroad that ran across the isthmus was completed, and the journey from New York City to San Francisco could be made in about a month.

The Mormons founded Salt Lake City in 1847, and it became a major arrival and departure point for the first overland mail service from Independence, Missouri. Soon after, a service was established from Salt Lake City to California. Mail originating in New York City took a month to get to Independence, another month to get from Independence to Salt Lake City, and about two more weeks to reach California. The Mormons in Salt Lake City were making an effort to colonize Los Angeles at the time, so they established a trail between the two cities. This was the route most used for mail in the winter, while the shorter and more northern route along the Humboldt River was used the rest of the year.

In the 1840s, the United States government justified its seizure of Texas, New Mexico, and Arizona by creating the Mexican-American

war. Once the war was won, with hardly a fight, the new citizens demanded a mail route. That route went from Independence, Missouri, over the Sante Fe Trail, to San Antonio, El Paso, and Santa Fe.

The amount the government paid carriers to operate a mail route didn't begin to pay for the expenses and the risks of the operation, so it took a long time to establish regular mail routes. During the 1850s, the public hue and cry grew steadily for a regular, reliable mail service between the coasts and into the vast new territories. Finally, in 1857, Congress passed a bill to establish an overland mail route.

The government contract to carry the mail across the country specified that the mail had to go twice a week, "performed with good four-horse coaches or spring wagons, suitable for the conveyance of passengers, as well as the safety and security of the mails." The first coaches headed west out of St. Louis and east out of San Francisco on September 15, 1858. To avoid the Rockies and northern winter weather, the route went circuitously, by way of western Arkansas; El Paso, Texas; Tucson, Arizona; Yuma and Los Angeles, California; and then north to San Francisco. The coaches took just over three weeks, logging 2,795 miles each way.

THE OVERLAND MAILMEN

The government awarded the overland mail route contract to the Overland Mail Company, a firm organized by several express companies, including Wells, Fargo & Co. The president from 1857 to 1860 was John Butterfield. A native of Utica, New York, Butterfield was enthusiastic and energetic, so much so that the route from St. Louis to San Francisco became known as the Butterfield Overland Mail. One of the primary stipulations of the contract was that the mail be delivered on time. Over and over again, Butterfield told his employees, "Remember boys, nothing on God's earth must stop the United States mail!" Despite an annual federal subsidy of $600,000, the Overland Mail lost heavily and Butterfield was replaced by William Dinsmore.

Independence, Missouri, founded in 1827 as a rendezvous point for fur traders, was a major staging point for emigrants to the West. This engraving (*top*) of the courthouse was done by Charles Dana in 1855.

William George Fargo (1818–1881) (*above*) was a dynamic, popular businessman. In conjunction with the shy and retiring Henry Wells he built Wells, Fargo and Co. into the leading express company in the West.

The first Pony Express rider (*above*) departed St. Joseph on April 3, 1860, amid great celebration and oratory.

The award of the overland mail contract was rife with politics. Postmaster Aaron Brown had originally awarded it to Jim Burch, founder of the California Stage Company and a millionaire by the age of 29. However, President Buchanan was a close friend of Butterfield, and overruled Brown. To appease Burch, he was authorized to operate a monthly overland route from San Antonio to San Diego.

The San Antonio to San Diego route was a particularly treacherous one, because the fierce Apache Indians ambushed the coaches whenever they found an opportunity. Most of the route was desert, and lack of water was an almost constant problem. Even with all the difficulties, Butterfield managed to create a well-organized operation. A station was built every ten to 15 miles and stocked with water, hay, grain, and food.

It wasn't long before other mail routes were approved. The Civil War closed down part of Butterfield's route, and in 1861 Congress awarded another contract for a central overland route to a firm called Russell, Majors & Waddell, who played a central part in transportation in the early West. Their Central Overland and Pike's Peak Express Company was organized in 1859 and ran from Leavenworth, Kansas to Denver, Colorado, to serve the Colorado gold rush. When the gold rush fizzled a few years later, the financial resources of the three men were strained, so they were glad for the government contract. The firm created the famous Pony Express to prove to the government that a daily route could be established. That was a suc-

In St. Joseph, Russell, Majors and Waddell selected the first floor of the town's newest hotel, Patee House, as their headquarters (*facing left*). The U.S. Postal Service provided a special mail railroad car, where the mail was sorted for the Pony Express. The car can still be seen at the Patee House.

cess, but the stagecoaches didn't fare as well, and the contract was sold at an auction in 1862 to Ben Holladay.

Holladay was a keen if unscrupulous businessman, determined to make his new venture work. He quickly went after other mail-route contracts and became known as the "Stagecoach King" and the "Napoleon of the Plains." Once Holladay had driven off most of his competitors, usually by a price war but occasionally by staging "Indian" attacks on them, fares rose astronomically. The luxurious Concord coaches were replaced by whatever Holladay could find. One passenger wrote, "There was of course no rebate of fare to passengers who had paid for first-class travel and had to put up with any conveyance Holladay chose to thrust upon them... The mud-bedaubed trips were so common they became a wry joke among the b'hoys who called them 'walking to Virginia City on the coach.'"

Only four years after Ben Holladay bought the Central Overland and Pike's Peak Express Company, he was bought out by Wells, Fargo & Co. This famed express and banking company had been in the business of buying up Western freight and stage lines for quite a few years, and the purchase of Holladay's business gave the firm a monopoly on all major stagecoach lines west of the Missouri River.

The stagecoach drivers of the first overland mail routes are some of the unsung heroes of American history. They had to have great courage and be extremely skilled drivers to steer four to six horses through every kind of weather, terrain, and poor road imaginable. Their long whips were an indispensable tool for keeping the horses under control, and probably for protection as well. Just as important was the person who rode shotgun and kept alert for hostile Indians and bandits, who were called road agents.

One of the more famous stagecoach drivers, or jehus as they were called, was "polite, profane, tobaccer chewin', cigar smokin' One-eyed Charlie." When One-eyed Charlie died and was laid to rest, they discovered he was a she!

Another romantic character of the stagecoach lines was Antoine Amedee Marie Vincent Manca de Vellombrusâ, Marquis de Morés. This French nobleman arrived in the Badlands in 1883. Among other ventures, he ran a feeder line near the gold mines of the Black Hills

Bronco Charlie (*top*), painted here in his old age, was a Pony Express rider. His wages were $25 a week.

The Pony Express (*middle*) ran only between St. Joseph, Missouri, and points west. Letters to and from points east went by United States Postal Service. This letter left San Francisco via Pony Express on October 17, arrived in St. Joseph on October 29, and in New York City a few days later.

A Pony Express letter (*bottom*) took the amazingly fast time of only ten days for delivery.

between Medora, North Dakota and Deadwood, South Dakota. It failed. The Marquis chose to ignore the U.S. Constitution and the outcome of the Civil War, and created a cattle ranch run like a feudal estate. Rumor has it he once challenged Theodore Roosevelt to a duel. He left Dakota for good in 1887 after being acquitted in a murder trial.

THE PONY EXPRESS

The courageous riders of the Pony Express captured the imagination of the American public as few events in American history have. The Pony Express was created by Russell, Majors and Waddell, a partnership that operated a huge freight and mail service between St. Joseph, Missouri and Sacramento, California.

Particularly in the days before railroads had penetrated the West, letters from home were a long time coming. In Denver in 1860, men lined up at the Central Overland California and Pikes Peak Express Company offices in the hope of mail (*above*).

A Wells, Fargo passenger coach (*right*) leaves Deadwood in 1890, pulled by six horses and carrying at least 15 people.

Ａ Wells, Fargo wagon (*left*) carrying $250,000 in gold from the great Homstake Mine prepares to leave Deadwood in 1890.

Ｓ tagecoach travel was scarcely luxurious. The dirt roads were rutted, rocky, and potholed. Where streams could not be forded they were crossed by rickety plank bridges like this one (*right*) over the Beaver Head River on the road between Ogden and Helena, Montana, in 1871.

Ｔ o the uninitiated, stage travel could be downright terrifying. This stagecoach (*below*) rounds a bend bordered by a precipitous drop on the road between Ouray and Red Mountain, Colorado, 1901.

Alexander Majors was the partner who was known as the "Prince of the Freighters." He wrote a book called Seventy Years on the Frontier that has many wonderful descriptions of life on a wagon train. The average freight wagon needed 12 oxen to pull it, and progressed at the speed of about two miles an hour. At one time Majors was using 3,500 wagons, 40,000 oxen, 1,000 mules and over 4,000 men. Those who drove the bulls had to walk beside them, and were known as "bullwhackers." These men were fairly low on the social totem pole of the frontier West, and had a reputation for foul language, tall tales, and gambling. However, Majors was a religious man, and would not tolerate cursing on his wagon trains. One of his ads for teamsters read, "The use of intoxicating liquors as a beverage, card playing and profane language are prohibited. Each man will be presented with a Bible and a hymn book."

Russell, Majors and Waddell wanted their mail contract to be expanded to a daily service. In 1860 William H. Russell made a trip to Washington, D.C. and with the help of a senator from California, who promised that they would be reimbursed, decided that a weekly Pony Express would prove that a daily overland mail route was feasible. Russell was that rare combination of dreamer and organizer, and he quickly talked his reluctant partners into spending the money on the creation of a pony express from St. Joseph, Missouri to San Francisco.

In 65 days the three men organized a 1,966–mile route that went over plains, mountains, and deserts – an almost unbelievably monumental task. The plan was for a weekly schedule of mail runs that would take ten days each way. Because the horses galloped all the way, they had to be changed every 12 to 15 miles. This meant that more than 119 relay stations were built. The stations also served as protection from marauding Indians. The well-rested, grain-fed mounts of the Pony Express could usually outrun the grass-fed mounts of the Indians. Five hundred sure-footed, fast, and tough ponies were purchased. It took 75 ponies to make the journey from

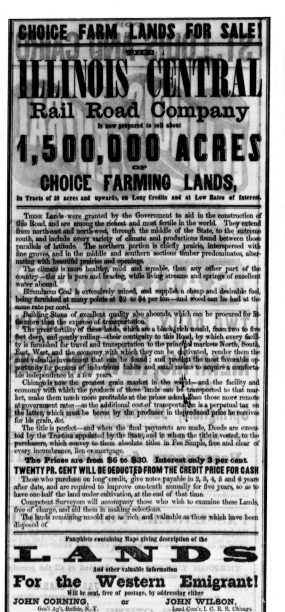

Railroad engineers were confronted by difficult natural challenges in the West. This trestle over Canyon Diablo in Arizona (*top left*), completed in 1903, is one example of how the challenge was met.

A mountain avalanche could destroy in moments the work of months, as the railroad builders found to their dismay. The solution was snow sheds to cover the tracks in the danger areas. Here (*left*) two construction workers stand on the roof of a snow shed built by the Central Pacific at Crested Peak, California, in 1860.

Building a railroad was enormously expensive. To help bring rail service to the West, Congress granted land to some railroad companies. The companies kept the land they needed and sold the rest. The first land grant railroad was the Illinois Central, completed in 1856. This poster (*above*) from the period advertises choice farmland for sale by the railroad.

Another example is the Marent Gulch viaduct, 226 feet high, built by the Northern Pacific west of Missoula, Montana in 1883 (*above*). Over a million board feet of lumber were used; it was torn down and replaced with an iron bridge two years later.

Building the railroads required thousands of laborers, who did backbreaking and often dangerous work. Particularly in California, where workers were scarce, the railroads often imported Chinese coolies to do the work. Recognizable by their distinctive round hats, here (*left*) they labor to build a trestle at Secrettown in the Sierra Nevadas for the Southern Pacific in 1877.

point to point. Each rider went from 45 to 75 miles before turning the route over to a fresh rider. The letters, wrapped in oiled silk to protect them from water, were carried in a leather mochila, a saddle-bag that was hung over the saddle and transferred from pony to pony.

Most of the Pony Express riders were boys. The advertisement for riders said the Pony Express wanted "young, skinny, wiry fellows not over 18." They had to be willing to risk death daily, and orphans were preferred. Indian attacks were common, and raids on the stations were the only thing that temporarily shut down the service. There were many tales of courage and resourcefulness in the face of in-credible danger and hardship.

Two riders named Holt and Wilson were at a relay station when about 80 Indians attacked it. When the riders' ammunition ran out the Indians broke down the door and demanded that the two riders take all the flour in the station and bake bread with it until it was gone. After the two had baked most of the day, the Indians tied them to a stake and piled sagebrush at their feet. Fortunately, another rider named William Dennis was due in from the West. He rode in, saw what was happening, and quickly rode a few miles back to where he had passed a column of 60 U.S. cavalry troops. Just as Holt and Wilson were about to become more baked than their bread, the cavalry charged over the hill, bugles playing and banners flying, and rescued them.

Another rider named Jim Moore was riding west with the mail. When he arrived at his station he discovered that the eastbound rider had been killed. He took the eastbound mail and, ten minutes after he had arrived, galloped back the way he had just come. He rode for 14 hours and 45 minutes over a distance of 280 miles, an extraordinary feat. A rider named Jack Keetley once rode west for 31 hours for a distance of 340 miles.

One of the most famous of the Pony Express riders was Robert Haslan, known as "Pony Bob." His home routes were between Lake Tahoe and a place called Buckland, 75 miles to the east. This route was right in the middle of Paiute Indian territory, and at the time the Paiutes were at war, enraged at the encroachments of the white man.

Frank Webner, a Pony Express rider, in 1861 (*above left*). In the 19 months the Pony Express existed, only one rider was killed by hostile Indians, and only one bag of mail was lost. The riders had covered 650,000 miles by horseback.

The Pony Express set up headquarters in the Patee House, the newest and best hotel in St. Joseph (*above right*).

The father of the famed Pony Express, Alexander Majors (1814–1900) (*below*). This short-lived venture lasted only 19 months and lost half a million dollars, but became part of American folklore.

An ox train used to transport supplies in Arizona Territory, 1883 (*left*).

This undated, obviously posed picture of Buffalo Bill (*below*) was probably taken as a publicity shot sometime in the 1880s.

On one heralded trip, Pony Bob started at the Tahoe station. Along the way he learned that the Indians were on the warpath and that many whites had already been massacred. At Buckland station the rider refused to go because of the danger. Pony Bob took the mail and, without resting, rode to Smith's Creek, 90 miles east of Buckland. He rested for nine hours, then rode west again. At a relay station some miles from Buckland, he discovered that the riders and station attendants had been killed, and the Indians had stolen the horses. He fed and watered his horse, and pushed on. At Buckland station he changed horses and rode to Tahoe. In all he had ridden 380 miles, with hostile Indians everywhere and with only nine hours of rest.

Pony Bob also rode the fastest trip of any Pony Express rider – 120 miles in eight hours and ten minutes, an average speed of 14.7 miles an hour.

Another famous Pony Express Rider was Will Cody. Cody's father died when he was 11, leaving him with a mother, five sisters, and a baby brother to support. He had a hard time finding work in Kansas, where the family lived, because they were anti-slavery in a pro-slavery area. Fortunately, Alexander Majors, of the freighting firm Russell, Majors and Waddell, was a friend of the family. He hired Will at a man's wages to herd cattle and run messages on his wagon trains. When he was about 14, Cody became caught up in the excitement of the Pikes Peak gold rush, and headed for Denver with a friend. They were young, inexperienced, and penniless, and soon turned back to Kansas.

A few months later, Cody was hired by the Pony Express. The wages were good, and he was valuable to them, being a good rider and experienced on the trail. His first route was 45 miles long, with two pony changes along the way. Later he was given a route that was 76 miles long, with the North Platte river to ford along the way. One day he was ambushed by Indians, and thought he had managed to outrun them to the next relay station. When he got there he discovered the Indians had already been there, killing the attendant and taking the ponies.

After some years serving in the Union Army, scouting, and shooting buffalo for railroaders, Cody was discovered by Ned Buntline, a writer of thrilling dime novels filled with heroic tales of the West. Cody made the perfect character for Buntline, who made him the hero of a sensational cheap novel in 1869, thus creating the character of Buffalo Bill. For the rest of his life, Will Cody lived his character. He acted in stage melodramas about the West in the winter, and worked as a scout or hunting guide in the summer. In 1883 he created Buffalo Bill's Wild West show, and became its star attraction. Though he had a reputation for being generous, he wasn't a good businessman, and let a couple of fortunes slip through his fingers. When he died in 1917 at the age of 71, he was ill and poverty-stricken; his Wild West show survived until 1932.

Buffalo Bill Cody (*top*) was famed as an Army scout. He is shown here (on the white horse) with General Nelson Miles, viewing a hostile Sioux camp near Pine Ridge, South Dakota, in early 1891.

Buffalo Bill with Chief Sitting Bull (*left*). In 1885 Sitting Bull actually toured for a season with the Wild West Show, maintaining a fierce dignity in the face of hostile crowds.

Promontory Point today is part of the Golden Spike National Historic Site. Exact replicas of the two original locomotives, the *Jupiter* (*facing top*) and *No. 119*, operate on nearly two miles of track laid on the original roadbed.

The Durango and Silverton narrow-gauge railroad (*facing bottom*) runs today between the two mining towns high in the Colorado Rockies. Constructing lines like this over the mountains required remarkable engineering ingenuity.

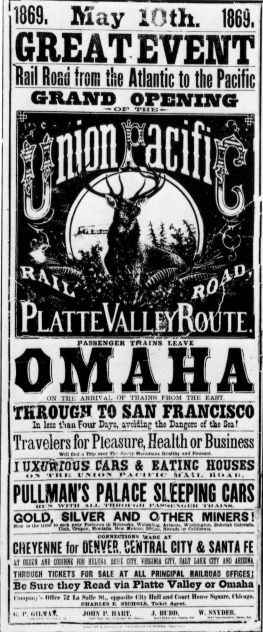

THE RAILROADERS

Once the overland mail routes were established, building a transcontinental railroad was the next logical step in improving transportation in the United States. The men who built the railroads were all strong characters; they were all visionaries, and some say, they were all slightly crazy.

Among the most obsessed of the railroaders was a man named Theodore Judah, a brilliant engineer who thought about nothing but railroads and how to build them for most of his life, which ended in 1868 at the early age of 38. He was commissioned to build a railroad from San Francisco to Sacramento, and then to survey a route over the Sierras to Nevada. From that point on he was obsessed with the idea of building a transcontinental railroad. He spent years trying to raise the money, lobbying in Washington, and planning the route. He finally hooked up with four businessmen who agreed to buy part of the stock in his company, and in 1862 Congress agreed to pay them by the mile to build the railroad. However, Judah was a scrupulously honest man, and his four partners were doing everything in their power, including changing maps, to bilk the government of its money. Judah was finally forced to sell out. The man who probably did more than any other to get a transcontinental railroad built died a few months later of yellow fever.

Judah's four partners were Collis P. Huntington, Mark Hopkins, Charles Crocker and Leland Stanford. Once they got rid of Judah, the Big Four, as they were later known, made the Central Pacific Railroad their own, and began to build eastward from Sacramento in earnest.

The other man who made an invaluable contribution to the building of the transcontinental railroad was Grenville M. Dodge. Born in 1831, Dodge had also been educated as an engineer in the East, and became a railroad fanatic at an early age. Like Judah, Dodge seems to have become a shrewd and dedicated salesman of the railroad early on. As he moved farther west, Dodge became more and more

The railroads of the West were often built in advance of the people who would use them. This camp (*above left*) of Union Pacific workers is at the end of the track near the Humboldt River Canyon in Nevada in 1868. A work train can be seen in the background.

The completion of the transcontinental railroad in 1869 was an epochal moment. As this Union Pacific poster (*above*) advertises, passengers could now travel from Omaha to San Francisco in luxurious Pullman cars in just four days.

enamoured of the outdoor life and the challenge of taming the land. His involvement with the transcontinental railroad began when in 1853 he ran a survey from Council Bluffs, Iowa to the foothills of the Rockies. He later surveyed the Platte River Valley and the Rockies on his own.

When Dodge went back to Council Bluffs he met Abraham Lincoln and shared with him his enthusiasm for a transcontinental railroad. At that point the Civil War broke out, and Dodge joined the Union Army as a colonel. Dodge distinguished himself in the Army and was awarded a general's star before returning to the West.

Finally, in 1862, the Pacific Railroad Act was passed by Congress, mandating that two railroads be built along the forty-second parallel: one west from Omaha and the other east from the Pacific Ocean. They would meet at an unspecified point.

In 1866 Dodge became chief engineer of the Union Pacific Railroad, which began building westward. Speed was essential to the building. The Union Pacific workers were recruited largely from rough Irish immigrants and Civil War veterans. Charles Crocker, who was in charge of construction for the Central Pacific, solved his labor problem by importing thousands of Chinese coolies. In either case, the rail workers lived in rowdy work camps that were aptly called "hell on wheels." The work progressed at breakneck speed (and often with little regard for the safety of the workers or the quality of the construction). On May 10, 1869, the two lines met at Promontory Point, Utah – over 1,000 miles west of Omaha. A symbolic golden spike was driven, and the nation was finally united by rail lines stretching from coast to coast.

Grenville M. Dodge (1831–1916) (*above*) became the chief engineer for the Union Pacific Railroad in 1866.

The Union Pacific Railroad and the Central Pacific Railroad met at Promontory Point, Utah (*below*), on May 10, 1869. A golden spike was driven to commemorate the event.

The force behind the Central Pacific and Southern Pacific railroads was Collis P. Huntington (1821–1900) (*below*).

THE OUTLAWS

Rounding up a horse thief, in what is very likely a
posed shot, in 1903.

The outlaws of the old West have become heroes in American history. This is ironic, since many of them were nothing more than ruthless, cold-blooded killers. Thousands of petty thieves and murderers were arrested during the frontier years. It was the men who escaped the law over and over again who became legends in their own time.

The Civil War spawned the majority of the outlaw gangs. Boys like the Younger brothers joined Confederate guerilla bands in their teens, and were exposed to murder as a way of life. When the Union won, their anger turned itself to the nearest handy target, which happened to be any kind of authority, and particularly any kind of Yankee authority. In spite of the fact that these outlaws killed many innocent people as casually as they would shake hands with them, they had much popular support among those who had supported the Confederacy. They were seen as modern-day Robin Hoods, robbing the rich to give to the poor. That these men robbed from the rich and poor to give only to themselves was ignored.

The Younger brothers, the James brothers, the Hole-in-the-Wall Gang, John Wesley Hardin and any number of other outlaws were, in effect, acting out the revenge fantasies of hundreds of thousands of people who had just lost a war, who had lost friends and relatives, and who had lost a way of life.

Frank James and Cole Younger got their first taste of the outlaw life while serving in the Civil War with Quantrill's Raiders, a band of Confederate guerillas. William Clarke Quantrill (1837–1865) taught his men the hit-and-run techniques they later used so successfully as criminals.

JOHN WESLEY HARDIN

In some ways the outlaw John Wesley Hardin epitomizes the tragedy of young boys forced into the role of men by a war that brought out the worst in everyone. He was born in 1853 in Texas, the son of a Methodist preacher and lawyer. His mother came from an educated, cultured family, and he was given a good education himself. In the atmosphere of lawlessness of Texas and the Civil War, Hardin began carrying a gun before he even reached puberty, and became known as an expert marksman by the time he was twelve.

Hardin killed his first man when he was 15, a black ranch hand who he claimed had tried to attack him with a club. For Hardin, this was the beginning of more than a decade of running from the law, and the first of more than 20 men that he killed. Hardin's father decided that there was no way his son would get a fair trial in a courtroom run by Yankees, and sent him off to live on a remote ranch with a friend. Union patrols came after him and he ambushed and killed three of them.

It seemed wherever Hardin went, he left dead men behind him. To hear his side of the story he was always the victim, always killing in self-defense. His family supported him in this viewpoint, as did most of Texas. As his reputation as a gunfighter grew there may have been some element of truth in this, since some cocky young cowboys challenged him. Throughout the years he spent running from the law, Hardin continued to try to get an education and be with his family. His cousin Manning Clements was a friend throughout his life. When he was 19, Hardin married Jane Bowen, the daughter of a rancher.

By the time he was 24 Hardin had killed more than 20 men, and in 1878 the law finally caught up with him. He served 14 years in Huntsville prison. His three children, Molly, Nan, and John Jr., grew up knowing their father only by his legend and the hundreds of letters he wrote their mother. Jane died while Hardin was in prison. When

Jesse James in his coffin. Jesse came to be seen as a Robin Hood figure who stole from the rich and gave to the poor. In reality, he was simply a bank robber and murderer.

he was released in 1892 Hardin had trained himself to be a lawyer. However, he was lonely, ill, weary, and bitter. Three years later, in 1895, he was shot in the back by the police chief of El Paso, who thought his act would enhance his reputation as a gunslinger. Hardin's killer, John Selman, was acquitted of the murder, but was himself murdered a few months later in a gunfight with a U.S. marshall named George Scarborough.

Jesse James began his outlaw career with a bank robbery at Liberty, Missouri, in February, 1866. His legendary criminal career continued until he was killed in 1882.

THE JAMES-YOUNGER GANG

Jesse and Frank James, and the Younger brothers, were also products of the Civil War. While not strictly outlaws of the frontier West, their exploits epitomized the lawlessness present at the time. Jesse was born in 1847; Frank was born in 1843. They grew up in Missouri, witnessing bloody battles between pro- and anti-slavery partisans in Kansas and Missouri before the war even began. When it did, Frank James and Cole Younger, the oldest of the Younger boys, joined Quantrill's Raiders, a band of Confederate guerillas so vicious and ruthless that they were outlawed even by the Confederacy. Jesse James joined an equally murderous guerilla band led by "Bloody Bill" Anderson.

Cole Younger had actually served in the regular Confederate Army with distinction, but when he was accused of murdering a man in Kansas he became a fugitive and his life of murder and robbery began. Jim and John Younger became caught up in their brother's trouble when they murdered four Union soldiers they believed were

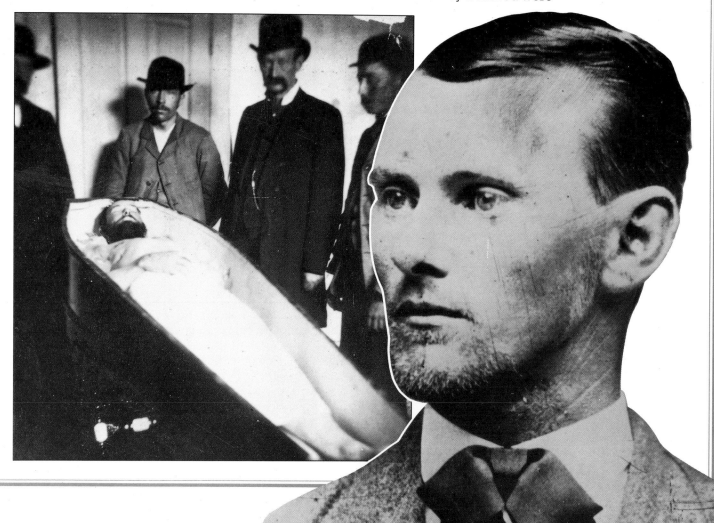

after Cole. After Quantrill's Raiders participated in a massacre in Lawrence, Kansas, described as one of the greatest atrocities of the war, the band dispersed. Cole fled to Texas and continued fighting for the Confederate Army.

When Cole returned to Missouri in 1865, just 21 years old, he was introduced to Jesse James. On February 13, 1866 12 men, led by Jesse and Cole, robbed the bank in Liberty, Missouri; a bystander was killed. Cole went to Texas afterward and took up with the famous Belle Shirley, known as Belle Star.

Over the next decade, Cole, Jim, John, and Bob Younger and the James brothers robbed dozens of banks and trains, always managing somehow to outwit the law and the Pinkerton detectives who were constantly on their trail. John Younger was killed in 1874, which inspired a fierce wave of murder and robberies by the gangs in reprisal.

Even as the Youngers and James murdered innocent people, they were becoming heroes. Theodore Roosevelt, under the mistaken impression that Jesse James was robbing from the rich to give the poor, called the outlaw the Robin Hood of America. The railroads were not popular in the late 1880s, run and owned as they were by wealthy men who were just as ruthless and cold-hearted as the outlaws, but who committed their crimes under the protection of their enormous wealth. The story was that the James family had been forced off their land and into poverty by the railroads (as had thousands of other people), and the James brothers' robberies were revenge. This myth was fueled when two Pinkerton detectives hired by the railroad tossed a bomb into the house where the mother and young half-brother of the James brothers were living, killing the half-brother and blowing off the mother's arm. Public sentiment turned to favor the outlaws, and they were often aided in their escapes by the citizenry.

In 1876 the James–Younger Gang made a fatal error when they decided to rob a bank in Northfield, Minnesota. This time the residents of Northfield turned on the outlaws. When they came out they were cut down by armed citizens who were determined to kill as many of the outlaws as they could. Two of the outlaws were killed and the rest were badly wounded. Those who hadn't been killed fled into a swamp, pursued by angry farmers. The Younger brothers had all been wounded, and after they refused to abandon brother Jim, whose jaw had been shot away, the James brothers left them to fend for themselves. The Younger brothers were captured and sentenced to life in prison. The James brothers barely managed to escape.

Bob Younger died in prison, but thanks to the efforts of a lawyer named Warren C. Bronaugh whose life Cole had saved during the war, Cole and Jim were pardoned in 1901. Jim committed suicide in 1902. Cole lived the rest of his life quietly, and died in 1916 at the age of 72.

After Northfield the James brothers went under false names to Nashville, Tennessee, intending to live quiet lives. But Jesse could never resist the temptation of a bank or a train with money in it and three years later they robbed a train in Missouri. When they murdered two men a short time later the Missouri governor put a price of $5,000 on each brother's head. In 1882 Jesse James was shot dead in his home in St. Joseph by Robert Ford – a member of Jesse's gang who had succumbed to the lure of a big reward. Frank James gave himself up soon after, but was never convicted for any crime. The

Frank James, Jesse's older brother (*top*), turned himself in a few months after Jesse was killed. He was tried three times for murder and robbery and found not guilty by sympathetic juries. He then lived quietly until his death in 1915.

Belle Starr (*above*) was one of a handful of legendary women outlaws. This engraving, which appeared in *The National Police Gazette* in 1886, shows Belle being cheered as she escapes arrest.

JESSE JAMES HOME

combination of public sentiment in Missouri and the fact that there was no clear-cut, solid evidence against him got him off the hook. He lived a quiet life and died in 1915 at the age of 72.

THE DALTON BROTHERS

The Dalton brothers were cut from the same cloth as the Younger brothers. James and Adeline Dalton were a Kansas and Missouri family. James was generally home from adventures in horse-trading and gambling only long enough to get Adeline pregnant. She gave birth to 15 children, 13 of whom lived. Of those, five formed an outlaw gang that robbed dozens of trains between Missouri and Colorado between 1890 and 1892.

The Dalton brothers made the same fatal error of judgement that the James–Younger gang had made when they decided to rob a bank in Coffeyville, Kansas. In fact, they decided to rob not one but two banks. It was a foolish move, because their faces were on wanted posters all over town. They were spotted by citizens outside the bank as soon as they went in. A local hardware store quickly armed every citizen willing to carry a gun; when the brothers came out they were ambushed. The only survivor was the youngest Dalton, Emmett. After he served his time in prison he moved to California and became a wealthy contractor.

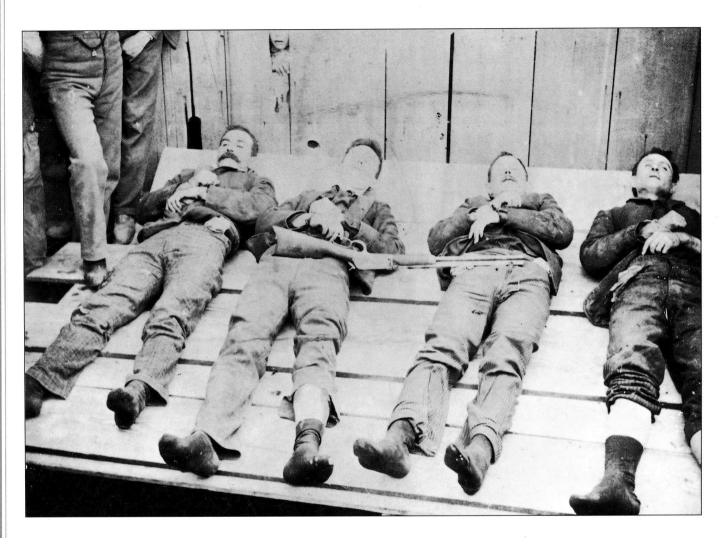

The Jesse James home (*top*) in St. Joseph, Missouri, can still be seen today. Jesse was killed here on April 3, 1882 by Bob Ford, a former associate.

Robert, Henrietta, Cole, and James Younger in a group portrait taken in 1889 (*facing bottom*).

BILLY THE KID

Henry McCarty, later known as Billy the Kid, has been depicted in American myth as a particularly cold-blooded killer, yet all the historical evidence is to the contrary. He was born in New York City probably in 1859. In the early 1870s his widowed mother, Catherine McCarty, moved to New Mexico with her two boys and soon remarried a miner. When Henry was 15 his mother died, and he moved in with some neighbors, doing menial chores in exchange for room and board.

When he was caught for petty theft in 1875 and thrown in jail, Henry made the first of his many jailbreaks and fled to Arizona, where he found work as a cowhand. Not long after he got to Arizona, at the age of 18, Henry shot a man in a saloon for calling him a dirty name. Again he was thrown in jail and escaped, this time returning to New Mexico and using the name William Bonney. He joined up with a cattle rustler named Jesse Evans. When that turned out to be not to his liking, Billy looked for other work, and eventually was introduced to a wealthy, cultured English rancher named John H. Tunstall. Tunstall took a shine to Billy, and hired him to work on his ranch, located near the town of Lincoln, New Mexico. It was at this point that Henry McCarty, alias William Bonney, became known as Billy the Kid.

On October 5, 1892, the members of the Dalton Gang decided to rob the two banks at Coffeyville, Kansas. Unfortunately for them, the citizens of Coffeyville were lying in wait. In the gun battle that followed, four of the five gang members (*above*) were killed (left to right): Bill Powers, Bob Dalton, Grat Dalton, and Dick Broadwell. Emmett Dalton was badly wounded.

Billy might have grown up to be another obscure cowhand in the frontier West, but he happened to be in Lincoln County just as the Lincoln County War was building up to its height. This so-called war was between two factions: the Murphy–Dolan faction, a group of corrupt politicians and cattle barons, and the Tunstall–McSween faction, a group of smaller ranchers and homesteaders with cattle baron John Chisum behind the scene. Thanks to his quick draw and sure aim, Billy had become the leader of Tunstall's cowhands. When Tunstall was brutally murdered in February of 1878, Billy, who had tried to stay out of the fray, took up arms with the Tunstall–McSween faction. In the months that followed Tunstall's murder, many men on both sides were murdered.

The showdown between the two factions occurred in July, 1878, with Billy's group holed up in some adobe buildings in the town of Lincoln, fighting off the so-called sheriff George Peppin and 40 deputies. The fight was a standoff until someone set fire to the houses. McSween and Billy tried to escape at night under cover of darkness and smoke. McSween was shot and killed, but Billy managed to ford the Ruidoso River and escape safely. This was, for all practical purposes, the end of the Lincoln County War.

After the Lincoln County War Billy found himself the leader of a gang, and turned to cattle-rustling and robbery. Like so many other young men of the era who became outlaws, much of his motive seemed to be in avenging the death of his friend Tunstall.

Meanwhile, a new governor had been appointed in New Mexico, General Lew Wallace, and he immediately declared amnesty for everyone involved in the Lincoln County War. Under the terms of the amnesty, Billy technically wasn't eligible because he was being sought for other murders. In spite of that he met secretly with the governor, who apparently promised him a full pardon if he agreed to testify against the killers of a lawyer named Chapman. Billy agreed to be arrested and held until the trial in 1879. Either the governor betrayed Billy, or was unable to help him. The Kid grew tired of waiting for his pardon and escaped from the jail.

A year after Billy escaped a man named Pat Garrett was appointed sheriff of Lincoln County. One of his first mandates was to capture Billy the Kid. Garrett caught Billy in 1880. The Kid was convicted of murder and sentenced to hang, but he managed to kill two deputies and escape. Garrett caught up with him again on the night of July 14, 1881, and killed him.

THE HOLE-IN-THE-WALL GANG

The Hole in the Wall Gang was a term loosely applied to a number of outlaw bands that roamed the American Southwest in the 1880s, hiding out in a desolate spot in northern Wyoming known as the Hole-in-the-Wall. Their other hideouts were Brown's Hole in the rugged area where the borders of Colorado, Utah, and Wyoming meet, and Robber's Roost. Among the most famous of this group were Tom McCarty, Laughing Sam Carey, Butch Cassidy, The Sundance Kid, Black Jack Ketchum, Kid Curry, and the Tall Texan (Ben Kilpatrick).

The Wild Bunch was the gang led by Butch Cassidy and Kid Curry. Between 1897 and 1901 the gang terrorized the Southwest, making major bank and train robberies, rustling cattle, and stealing horses. There seems to have been a core group of about ten men who rode

O f all the legendary outlaws, perhaps Billy the Kid tops the list. He seems to have liked guns even before turning outlaw. Here (top) he poses (upper left) with five fellow members of a gun club in the early 1870s.

S heriff Pat Garrett (1850– 1908) (above) pursued Billy the Kid and his companions for months before he finally killed the Kid on July 14, 1881.

M uch about Billy the Kid is unknown, including his real name and date of birth. Most historians claim he was born as Henry McCarty, but others say his real name was William H. Bonney. This picture of Billy (facing) holding a carbine was taken around 1879.

Black Jack Ketchum being fitted with a new necktie (*above*). He was hanged at Clayton, New Mexico Territory, in 1901.

General Lew Wallace (*below*), better known as the author of *Ben Hur,* was territorial governor of New Mexico while Billy the Kid was a wanted man.

together in the Wild Bunch during those years. The others either dropped out, were killed, or got the money they wanted and settled down to respectable lives.

Butch Cassidy's real name was Robert Leroy Parker. He was born in Utah in 1866. His grandfather, Robert Parker, immigrated from England and was one of the leaders of the Mormon Hand Cart Expedition in 1856. His son Maximilian, who had a horse ranch and guided Mormon wagon trains from the midwest to Utah, was the father of the famous outlaw. The alias Cassidy apparently came from a cowhand on the Parker ranch who was a great friend of Robert Leroy as he grew up. Butch Cassidy joined up with a gang of outlaws led by Tom and Bill McCarty when he was about 17. After robbing a few banks, including the First National Bank in Denver, he apparently went straight for a while, then was arrested for stealing horses in 1894. After serving 18 months of a two-year term in a Wyoming penitentiary, Butch was released. Cassidy was next heard from at the Hole-in-the-Wall, where he quickly became the leader of an outlaw band that came to be called the Wild Bunch. Here he met Harry Longbaugh (alias the Sundance Kid).

The women associated with the Wild Bunch were characters in their own right. Etta Place is described as a beautiful woman with reddish hair. Some historians depict her as a lonely schoolmarm who fell in love with the dashing Sundance Kid, and others depict her as a prostitute, who enjoyed the outlawry of her main man. After they had pulled off a major robbery the Wild Bunch often went to Fanny Porter's Sporting House, a bordello in southern Texas. It's thought that Etta came from Fanny's.

Annie Rogers, who also worked in Fanny's house, was the sweetheart of Kid Curry. Curry's pattern seems to have been to pull off a robbery, stop off at Fanny's Place to pick up Annie, and travel around America in high style until the next job. She was arrested for passing forged bank notes, but was released after Kid Curry (who had been captured) signed a statement swearing that she didn't know his true identity or that the papers were forged. Shortly after she was released Annie returned to Texas and then disappeared.

Laura Bullion, also known as Della Rose, was the Tall Texan's lover. Both of them were arrested in St. Louis and she served a five-year jail term. When she was released she opened a boarding house in St. Louis.

Eventually most of the Wild Bunch had been killed or jailed. Things got too hot for Butch Cassidy and the Sundance Kid, and in 1901 they decided to move with Etta Place to South America. (Etta returned to America alone in 1906 and vanished from history.) They began respectably enough as ranchers near Buenos Aires, but by 1906 they could no longer resist going back to the business they knew best. They began robbing trains and banks in South America. Finally, in 1911, they made a fatal mistake, robbing the payroll for a mine in the valley of San Vincente, Bolivia. They also took a silver donkey, rode it back into town, and tied it outside a hotel. The donkey was well-known by the villagers as belonging to the foreman of the mine. They quickly found out what had happened, and summoned troops who surrounded the hotel. By morning the Sundance Kid had been killed, and Cassidy finally committed suicide when he realized he was hopelessly outnumbered and surrounded.

THE LAWMEN

The O.K. Corral in Tombstone, Arizona. The famous shootout here between the Earps and the Clantons on October 25, 1881 remains controversial to this day. Did the Earps do their duty as law officers, or did they shoot down unresisting innocents?

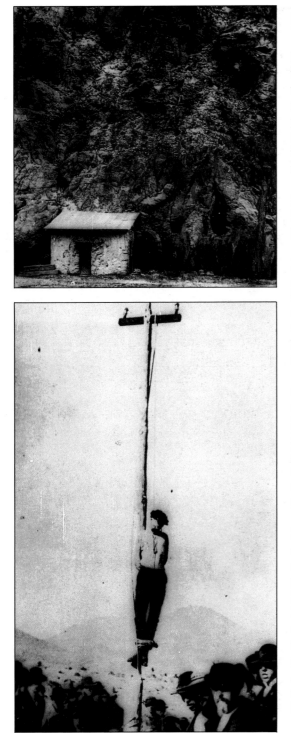

The jail at Clifton, Arizona (*top*), was built around 1881 by blasting cells into the face of a cliff. The first prisoner was also the builder, a Mexican who was jailed for a "shooting up" celebration.

The lynching of John Heith (*above*) at Tombstone, Arizona, in 1884. He was implicated in a store robbery in which four people were killed. His five confederates were apprehended and legally hanged at Tombstone a month later.

On the American frontier there were often a very fine line or none at all between outlaws and lawmen. Most of the cow towns and mining towns of the West were simply grateful to have someone brave enough to strap a pair of six-shooters to his waist and maintain some semblance of law and order. A sheriff who wore a tin badge one day might be swinging from a tree for cattle rustling the next, lynched by the very people whose lives he was protecting – and whose cattle he was stealing. An outlaw in one town might ride on to another and become sheriff. A sheriff might decide it was more profitable to join a band of cattle rustlers, and moonlight until he was caught and run out of town.

There were, however, honest and upright lawmen in the old West. Bill "Uncle Billy" Tilghman (1854–1924) was an intelligent, resourceful, and persistent lawman who chased the Doolin Gang, the Dalton Gang, and the Starr Gang, contributing to the demise of all three.

Charlie Siringo began his career as a cowboy in Texas in 1871. In 1885, at the age of 30, he published the first cowboy autobiography: A Texas Cowboy, or, Fifteen Years on the Hurricane Deck of a Spanish Cow Pony. This immensely popular book was reprinted dozens of times. In 1885 he joined the Pinkerton Detective Agency, and spent the next 25 years chasing outlaws. Siringo was largely responsible for the capture of many members of the Wild Bunch. He continued to write books about his life until his death in 1928.

"Bear River" Tom Smith didn't drink, gamble, or use his gun unless absolutely forced to. He was mild-mannered and spoke softly. Smith established his reputation for courage and coolness under fire in Bear River, Wyoming in 1868. In 1870 he became marshal of Abilene, Kansas, keeping the wild town under control by using only words, backed up by his fists. Just four months after he was appointed sheriff, Smith was serving a warrant on a pair of homesteaders accused of murder. One shot him, and the other split his skull with an ax.

The next man to become sheriff of Abilene was James Butler, better known as Wild Bill Hickock, another man of dubious skill and morality made famous by journalists. Hickock was a crack shot, and didn't object to using his guns. In 1861 he killed three men in a quarrel, a number later dime novels exaggerated to ten and even 30. He once claimed to have killed over 100 men, "all for good reasons." Hickock concocted fabulous lies about his adventures on the frontier, usually making himself out to be a hero when in reality he had been treacherous or cowardly. His reputation as a gunfighter, aided by his own bragging and the work of imaginative publishers, grew rapidly. After eight months as sheriff of Abilene, Hickock became a drifter, earning a living as a gambler and lawman; he also appeared with Buffalo Bill's Wild West show.

In 1876 in Cheyenne he married Agnes Lake Thatcher, a circus performer, but left her within a matter of months to go to Deadwood in Dakota Territory, where gold had been discovered. He was playing cards in a saloon on August 2, 1876 when a young drifter named Jack McCall, who wanted to be known as a great gunfighter, walked in and shot Hickock in the back of the head.

The lawmen who did survive, and who did keep their integrity, went out of their way to avoid trouble and violence. This may be a key difference between those sharpshooters of the old West who became outlaws, and those who became lawmen.

The law west of the Pecos. In this famous photo, Judge Roy Bean (seated on a beer keg and wearing a sombrero) tries a horse thief at his rough-and-ready court at his saloon in Langtry, Texas, in 1900. There were no other peace officers in the locality at the time.

It seems that incorruptible lawmen were the exception rather than the rule. Most often they were well paid to look the other way at atrocities committed by cattle barons who were willing and able to kill to rid themselves of unwanted sheepherders and homesteaders. For a lawman to stay alive in the frontier West took a peculiar combination of skill with a gun, nerves of steel, and downright paranoia. Once a lawman had established a reputation for being tough, he was marked as a living target by young outlaws who thought to enhance their reputation as gunfighters by shooting him down.

Many of these combination outlaws and lawmen were itinerant gamblers who were probably forced to move from town to town to support their addiction to taking risks, both at the gambling tables and with their own lives. Those who tried to marry and settle down usually found themselves moving on within a few years.

Much of what motivated these men to become the law was egotism. The sheriff was a central and powerful figure in every frontier town. He *was* the law, and often interpreted it to suit his needs. Sheriffs were usually reasonably well paid (the more famous lawmen could virtually name their fee), and often owned saloons, hotels, brothels, and gambling houses.

BAT MASTERSON

Bat Masterson was born in 1853 and grew up in Kansas. After a job on the railroad in his late teens, Masterson became a buffalo hunter in 1873. Like most of the best-known lawmen of the West, Masterson was renowned for his markmanship from a relatively young age. After serving as a scout for the Army, prospecting, and running a gambling table, Bat went to Deadwood, Dakota Territory, where he was persuaded by his friend Wyatt Earp to run for sheriff of Ford

Tombstone's city hall (*above left*), erected in 1882. Tombstone lives on today as a well-preserved pocket of Western history.

Silver was discovered in the San Pedro Valley, seventy miles west of Tucson, Arizona, in 1877. The miners who poured into the town of Tombstone swelled the population to 10,000. By 1882 lawlessness was so widespread that President Chester A. Arthur threatened to impose martial law. The Cochise County Court House in Tombstone (*above right*), built in 1882, was a busy place.

Every Tombstone should have an epitaph. The Tombstone *Epitaph* was founded in 1881. The newspaper offices (*right*) can still be seen.

The interior of the Cochise County Court House (*above*), little changed from October 25, 1881, when Virgil Earp arrested Ike Clanton and brought him here to appear before the justice of the peace – an event that led directly to the shoot-out at the O.K. Corral.

Ladies of joy were numerous in Tombstone in the 1880s. Many also worked as performers at the Bird Cage Theatre (*left*). The theater was owned during that period by Joe Bignon and his wife, who performed as well. She was billed as "Big Minnie: six feet tall and 230 pounds of loveliness in pink tights."

Dodge City, Kansas, in the 1870s. This rip-roaring cattle town had a reputation for violence, but in fact few gun battles actually took place there.

County. When he was elected, in 1877, he was only 24 years old, but "bad with a pistol."

Masterson quickly became an American legend. The small, neat man was a courageous and competent lawman who took his job seriously. He served for two years, then went to Leadville, Colorado and gambled; from there he went in 1881 to Tombstone, Arizona and joined his friend Wyatt Earp. He ran a faro table there, until the famous "showdown at the O.K. Corral." Next he went to Los Animas, Colorado, where he operated a faro table and then became a deputy sheriff.

During these years of wandering, gambling, and gunfighting, Bat was in and out of Dodge City frequently. Eventually, in the late 1880s, he settled in Denver, where he bought the gaudy Palace Variety Theater and Gambling Parlors. In 1891 he married singer and dancer Emma Walters, and soon after went to Creede, Colorado, the scene of a major silver strike. Creede was a crowded, violent, dirty city at the time; unlike many other lawmen of the time, Bat refused to participate in the violence. In fact, Masterson always chose the path of least violence, becoming known for clubbing attackers on the head with his pistol, or beating them with his cane, rather than shooting them. Creede became tiresome fast and Masterson soon returned to Denver. In the early 1890s he began writing a sports column and became involved in the world of boxing – and in the unsavory gamblers associated with it. He also began to drink heavily.

In 1902 Bat and Emma moved to New York City, where they lived for the rest of their lives. He became a prominent newspaper columnist and had many well-known friends, including Theodore Roosevelt. He died at his desk in 1921.

WYATT EARP

Wyatt Earp's reputation as a hero and lawman of the frontier West seems to have a lot to do with the fact that he had a good biographer and knew many of the famous lawmen and outlaws of the day. When his career is seen next to someone like Bat Masterson or Bill Tilghman, he looks to be treading that fine line between lawman and outlaw.

Wyatt Earp was born in Illinois in 1848, and moved to California with his family in 1864, when he was 16 years old. When he was in his early twenties he returned to the plains and drifted from place to place. He was arrested in Indian Territory in 1871 for stealing horses, but escaped; in 1872 he was a buffalo hunter. In 1875 he became a deputy sheriff in Wichita, Kansas, and a year later in Dodge City. He established himself as a crack shot in these years, and made friends with people like Wild Bill Hickock and Bat Masterson. By 1879 Dodge had become a quiet town, and Wyatt headed for Tombstone, Arizona. He persuaded his brothers to join him there. Wyatt worked as a Wells, Fargo guard; James became a bartender; Virgil was soon appointed town marshall. A year later brother Morgan took over Wyatt's job; Wyatt became deputy sheriff. Wyatt also ran the gambling tables at the Oriental Saloon. Doc Holliday, a friend of Wyatt, also joined him.

Doc Holliday was neither a lawman nor an outlaw, strictly speaking, but he managed to get himself into a lot of trouble and make a name for himself. He was a young dentist practicing in Atlanta when doctors told him he had tuberculosis, and only a few years to live. He moved West for the dry air, but ironically spent most of the rest of his life in the fetid atmosphere of saloons and gambling houses. He found he had a knack for gambling, and became a professional, appearing in most of the major cow towns and mining towns of the West before he finally died in 1887, 15 years after he had been given only a few years to live.

Dodge City, Kansas peace commissioners in 1890 (left to right): Charlie Bassett, Bill Harris, Wyatt Earp, Luke Short, L. McClean, Bat Masterson, and Neal Brown.

Doc Holliday might have remained just an obscure gambler, but he became the sidekick of Wyatt Earp and participated in the famous showdown at the O.K. Corral. Holliday wasn't an easy man to get along with: he drank too much, he was probably involved in some robberies, and he certainly killed his share of men.

It was the Earp brothers, along with Doc Holliday, Bat Masterson, and Luke Short, who came up against a group of cowboys and cattle rustlers who had been running Tombstone in their own lawless way. A long chain of events led to the famous gunfight at the O.K. Corral in 1881, which led to a bloody string of revenge murders and treachery on both sides. When Virgil was wounded and Morgan was killed, Wyatt crossed the line and became a killer, out for vengeance. After shooting the men he believed responsible for his brother's death, Wyatt and Doc Holliday headed for Colorado.

Both Wyatt and Virgil operated saloons and gambling halls in Colorado and California through the 1890s. When the Alaska gold rush began, Wyatt opened a saloon in Nome in 1897. Virgil died of pneumonia in 1906. Wyatt returned to southern California and Arizona the same year. From that point his life was a fairly quiet one of modestly profitable business ventures. He died in 1929.

Charley Storms was killed by Luke Short in February 1881 in a quarrel over a faro game (*top left*). Short was frequently called the "undertaker's friend."

George Johnson innocently bought a stolen horse and suffered the consequences (*right*).

Although the coroner's jury exonerated the Earps, the citizens of Tombstone had no doubts about the justice of the shootout at the O.K. Corral (*top right*).

The cemetery at Tombstone (*above*) was laid out in 1878 and used until 1884, when another cemetery was opened. It is a true symbol of this roaring mining town in the 1880s. The five men buried here were responsible for the Bisbee Massacre, where four innocent bystanders were killed during the robbery of a store owned by Arizona Senator Barry Goldwater's grandfather.

WOMEN OF THE OLD WEST

A prostitute named Margarita is one of many
buried in Tombstone's Boothill cemetery. She
was stabbed by Gold Dollar, another prostitute, in a
quarrel over a man in the 1880s.

The pupils in a one-room schoolhouse were most likely to be taught by a woman. This teacher and her pupils posed in front of their sod schoolhouse in Oklahoma Territory, around 1895.

During the time the American West was being settled by white pioneers, women were considered by society in general to be weak and in need of protection from all physical, mental, and emotional hardship. The reality was that most women couldn't afford that luxury. Those who were pioneers had to cope with whatever came along. Life was tough, even brutal, in the raw, unpopulated, and uncivilized West of the 1800s.

In many ways, the women who went West are the great, unsung heroes of the American saga. There seems to be a popular notion that women of the old West were either prostitutes or wives and mothers. In truth, women played a great variety of roles, according to their needs or the needs of their families. In the often harsh environment of the West, rules were set aside in favor of practicality more often than not.

Sometimes the men of the family would go West first and get somewhat settled before sending for the women. The first single woman in a mining town was likely either to get married right away or become a prostitute. Either way, she would play the role of wife, mother, doctor, cook, washerwoman, confessor, and banker for any number of men. The married women might limit their role as wife to one man, but were equally likely to be ministering to a whole community of men in many roles.

The pioneer women raised children in extremely primitive conditions, usually tending livestock and gardens at the same time they were coping with the cooking, sewing, cleaning, and all the other infinite chores that go with being a housewife. Husbands were usually off plowing, planting, herding, hunting, or mining. Often the men of the family would go off for months at a time to work for the railroad, cut timber, or do any number of jobs that would bring in some cash. Marauding Indians were a constant threat, as were any kind of illness or accident that required more than rudimentary medical care. They had to know how to shoot a gun, and how to care for the sick and injured – animals as well as people.

A pioneer woman had to be physically strong, mentally resource-ful, and emotionally tough just to survive from day to day. It was no wonder that when a handful of women did appear in a new town they banded together, even going so far as to build their houses close together, forming an important support system for each other.

Women also tended to have a so-called "civilizing" influence wherever they went. They started schools, churches, and temperance societies. They were more likely to insist on creating some form of law and order, and setting sanitation standards for the growing towns. They attracted more in the way of merchants, peddlers, preachers, and doctors. In fact, it was the women of Wyoming who secured for themselves the first vote for women any-where. In 1869 they were invested with "all the political rights, duties, franchises, and responsibilities of male citizens."

SHADY LADIES

For every town that sprang up along the railroad, near a gold or silver strike, a military fort, or an important trail junction, there were women who appeared as prostitutes and gamblers. There is a popu-lar notion that the majority of these women quickly married and became respectable wives and mothers. Most evidence says other-wise. It is estimated that there were at least 50,000 "bawds" working their way around the towns of the American West from the mid- to late-1800s, when prostitution was legal. Many a fortune in gold and silver went to these women, who saw no reason to trade their relative freedom, wealth, and comfort for the hardship of maintaining a home and family. In truth, the numbers were probably much larger than 50,000, given that there were at least 10,000 "strumpets" in San Francisco alone.

The down side of prostitution in the West is that many bordellos were breeding grounds for alcoholism, drug addiction, suicide, disease, and poverty. Where there was a red-light district there

Thirsty cowboys settle the dust at a bar in Old Tascosa, Texas, in 1908.

were saloons and gambling halls, both tending to create an atmosphere of violence. Brawls and murders were not uncommon in the red-light districts. Many of these women aged rapidly and found themselves out on the streets, poverty-stricken, diseased, and unable to care for themselves. Even in the old West they were judged harshly by society, and suicide was often the way out for women who felt helplessly stuck.

When the morals of the Victorian East were brought West, the consequences could be fatal for women who had changed the rules of society to suit themselves. There are two known stories of women who were lynched for breaking cultural taboos. Both owned ranches in cattle country. Elizabeth Taylor in Clay County, Nebraska reputedly sold her body in return for labor on her ranch. Ella Watson of Wyoming supposedly traded her favors for maverick cattle brought in by neighboring cowboys.

LADY OUTLAWS

There were also women outlaws, who gave the law just as much trouble as their male counterparts. Annie McDougal, called Cattle Annie, and Jennie Metcalf, known as Little Britches, were allegedly involved in just about every illegal activity the era had to offer, including peddling whiskey to the Indians, rustling horses and cattle, highway robbery, and bank robbery. When they were finally apprehended they were sent East to a reform school. It is said that Little Britches found religion and died in poverty in New York City, and Cattle Annie moved back to Oklahoma and became a solid citizen.

Little is actually known about the Rose of the Cimarron, whose real name was either Rosa Dunn or Rose O'Leary. Legend has it that she fell in love with the outlaw George Newcombe, known as Bitter Creek, and left a life of respectability to be with him. It is said that during a gunfight in Ingalls, Oklahoma in which her lover was trapped, she crossed a street flying with bullets with a rifle hidden under her skirts, allowing him to make his escape.

POKER ALICE

The Wild West had its fair share of lady gamblers, many becoming legends in their own time. Some of them were Madame Moustache, Faro Nell, Haltershanks Eva, Iowa Bull, and Prairie Rose. These women had to be street-smart and have nerves of steel to make a living gambling. One of the most famous and resourceful of these women was Poker Alice.

Alice Ivers was definitely her own woman, making up her own rules as she went through life. She was born in England, educated in a seminary by her schoolmaster father, and immigrated to the United States with her parents when she was a teenager. They came out West with the silver rush, and soon after Alice married a miner named Frank Duffield. They settled in Lake City, a town near Leadville. Gambling was a major form of entertainment in the early mining towns, and Alice just happened to take a shine to the game. She spent hours at home practicing every game she knew, and when her husband came home from work they would go out and gamble.

When Frank died, Alice decided to strike out on her own. It may be that she didn't have many other options; it may be that she had

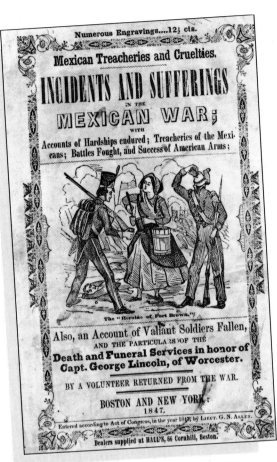

The heroine of the battle of Fort Brown was Mrs Sarah Borginnis, who served hot coffee to the soldiers when they were besieged by Mexican troops at Brownsville, Texas, in May of 1846. Known affectionately as The Great Western, she was known far and wide for her cooking, nursing, and loving.

Poker Alice led a long and colorful life as a gambler in the mining towns of the West.

been bitten by the gambling bug and knew she was good at it. She began her career with cards in Lake City, but soon got restless and began to move around the Colorado mining towns, a .38 pistol strapped to her hip. This is when she started becoming known as Poker Alice. When her winnings totaled $6,000, Alice made a bee-line for New York City and lived the good life for as long as her money lasted. She returned to the West, decked in the latest satin gowns, and drifted from town to town, depending on where the gambling action was.

Alice married twice after she returned from New York City; both men died within a few years of the marriage. After her third husband died Alice began looking for a more settled life, with or without marriage, and opened a combination brothel and casino near Fort Meade, South Dakota. For years she was a fixture in the Dakotas.

When prostitution and gambling were outlawed, she retired. She died during gall bladder surgery in 1930, at the ripe old age of 79.

THE CAMP FOLLOWERS

Another breed of old West shady ladies were the camp followers. These women followed army camps, mining camps, railroad camps, or wherever large groups of transient men were assembled in one place. Although these women were much appreciated by the men at the moment, theirs was usually an independent, risky, and lonely lot.

One of the most famous of the camp followers from the early 1840s to the late 1860s was Mrs. Sarah Borginnis, known as The Great Western. She was said to be over six feet tall with red hair, blue eyes, and a fair complexion. It was also said that this formidable woman could hold her own in a fight.

In spite of her tough side, The Great Western became known as a camp follower for her acts of kindness and understanding. She was truly one of those pioneer women who served as a lover, mother, wife, cook, laundress, and confessor to many men. She first gained attention when she brought hot food and drinks to the men engaged in a battle at Fort Texas. She kept restaurants for the men, and was known as a great nurse. She married enlisted men with frequency, apparently as a way to stay with the camps legally. Finally, The Great Western settled near Fort Yuma and opened a restaurant, which she ran until her death at the age of 53.

THE GREAT MADAMS OF DENVER

Every town and city of the old West had its red-light district with concomitant stories of the madams, their girls, and their customers. There were far more men than women on the frontier, many of them making and losing fortunes overnight in the gold and silver mines, and many brothels did a booming business.

Denver was among the largest and most lawless of the boom towns during the 1880s. The population went from a few thousand to a hundred thousand in a couple of years, and the mines kept producing what must have seemed like an infinite supply of wealth. Denver's red-light district on Durant Avenue was infamous throughout the West for its size and its violence. Naturally, a few women rose to the top of the heap as the queens of the red-light district, and gained their own unique kind of notoriety.

The queen of queens was a woman named Mattie Silks, probably one of the most famous madams of the old West. She started her career as a bad and beautiful woman at the tender age of 19, operating a "boarding house for young ladies" in Springfield, Illinois. When things got a bit hot for her in Illinois, she moved west to Kansas. When she was run out of Kansas, she started working the cattle towns. Eventually, she found a town that welcomed her with open arms, made her feel at home, and made her wealthy – Denver, Colorado.

Mattie is usually described as a miniature version of Lily Langtry, with blonde hair, blue eyes, and a peaches-and-cream complexion. One of her trademarks was a collection of dresses, always in the latest fashion, with two pockets in every one. In one pocket she carried an ivory-handled pistol, in the other gold coins.

Mattie first gained fame for the only known duel between two women. The issue at stake was supposedly a man named Cort Thompson, a slick, tall, blond Texan with a curled moustache who Mattie was in love with for most of her life. The other woman, a rival madam named Katie Fulton, was apparently making a play for Cort's attentions. As it turned out, Cort acted as Mattie's second. The women paced off, counted to three, turned, and fired. When the dust and smoke had cleared, both women had gotten away without a scratch, but Cort had been nicked in the neck. Some speculated that a jealous Katie Fulton decided that if she couldn't have him, nobody could, and deliberately aimed at him.

Cort was Mattie's "solid man" for many years, and eventually they were married. She had plenty of cash to spend, and much of it went to support her man, who wasn't inclined to work. What wasn't spent on Cort was spent on a racing stable, a pasttime she enjoyed for many years.

Mattie Silks had many adventures in her years as Denver's main madam. When Denver was courting a visiting railroad tycoon he was presented with the keys to the city and the keys to Mattie's house. He fell head over heels for Mattie, and proposed that she take a month off and accompany him to San Francisco. She ended up spending two months with the man, with the blessing and encouragement of the Chamber of Commerce and her husband. She was introduced as his wife, and taken to all the fancy society balls and parties. In the end she didn't win the railroad for Denver, but she had a great time trying.

When gold was discovered in Alaska, Mattie and Cort couldn't resist cashing in on it themselves. In three months they had bank-rolled $38,000, and were headed back to Denver before winter set in.

The woman who came closest to rivaling Mattie Silks as queen of the red light districts was a tall, cultured woman called Jennie Rogers, who came from St. Louis and had a sense of taste and style that Mattie never had.

When Jennie arrived from St. Louis she promptly purchased a house on the "row" from Madame Silks, and proceded to redecorate it completely from top to bottom. Every five or six weeks Jennie received a visit from her sweetheart, who Denver soon discovered to be the chief of police of St. Louis. It wasn't long before she had purchased a total of three houses that were dazzling in their elegance. Jennie's trademarks were her emerald earrings, and the matched pair of bay horses which took her for an airing in a fancy two-wheeled trap every afternoon.

CALAMITY JANE

Martha Canary, later known as Calamity Jane, was born in Missouri in 1852. When she was 12 her family moved to Montana. From that point on her history is fuzzy, and changes from historian to historian. The theme that does run through all descriptions of her is that although Calamity Jane had a serious drinking problem for most of her life, she was well loved by those who knew her.

Supposedly her parents died when she was still fairly young, and she ended up working as a dishwasher at Fort Bridger, Wyoming, which is where the name Calamity Jane began. Other accounts say

Calamity Jane on horseback in 1901, probably taken while she was appearing as an attraction at the Buffalo Pan-American Exposition.

she grew up with her parents, but being in the Wild West, learned to smoke, shoot a gun, and ride a horse – none of which were considered ladylike behaviour in those days. Stories have her as a mule-skinner, a scout for General Custer, and a teamster. There is some evidence that she turned to prostitution when necessary. It is known that she was in the Black Hills of Dakota Territory from 1876 to 1880 during the peak gold-rush period; from 1880 to 1895 she drifted across Kansas, Montana and Wyoming.

Though there are no formal records, Calamity Jane called herself Mrs. M.E. Burke for many years, and it is fairly certain that she lived with a hack driver named Clinton Burke. Some accounts say she had a child and gave it away as soon as it was born, while other accounts say she had a daughter who she put in a boarding school when she was a teenager.

There are persistent, though unproven, rumors that Calamity Jane was secretly married to, or had an affair with, Wild Bill Hickock.

Calamity Jane had a natural talent for theater, a talent she plied on and off for years from 1896 on with various Wild West shows, where she was billed as "The White Devil of Yellowstone." Unfortunately, she could never stay sober long enough to hold a job. She died in 1903 at the age of 51, and was buried next to Wild Bill Hickock in Deadwood, South Dakota.

RELIGION, CULTURE AND JOLLIFICATION

St. Paul's Episcopal Church in Virginia City,
Nevada. Built during the city's heyday in the 1870s,
the church is one of the oldest Episcopal churches
in the West.

I n the frontier West, entertainment could take the form of a Sunday sermon, an intellectual debate on the immortality of the soul, or at the other end of the spectrum, a hurdy-gurdy dance hall full of shady ladies and gamblers.

Preachers were scarce in the West, and a sermon was an excuse to gather and socialize. (The exception to this was in New Mexico and California, where Spanish missionaries had already been settled for 300 years.) Most preachers welcomed all denominations, and rode a circuit of towns. Other preachers ordained themselves, went West with a wagon train as the resident clergyman, then abandoned the clerical collar for more profitable enterprises when they reached their destination.

Mission San Xavier del Bac in Tucson, as photographed in 1871 (*facing top*). The church, built between 1779 and 1797, is considered the finest example of Spanish colonial architecture in America. The bell tower at right has never been finished.

Indians and whites attend Sunday school together in Indian Territory, Oklahoma, in 1900 (*facing bottom*).

Harry Patton of the Three Block Ranch in New Mexico enjoys his music in a division camp around 1905 (*above*).

The E. Romero Hose Company (*below*) demonstrating their fire-fighting skills in Las Vegas in 1889.

Sermons were held in whatever home, hotel, or saloon would hold the worshippers. In some areas the event of a gathering was used as an excuse to sell whiskey and women as the people left the service.

Another major form of "clean" entertainment was a lyceum, or cultural society, usually a loosely knit organization that sponsored debates, lectures, literary discussions, and sometimes, a singing society. These gatherings were more for the purpose of socializing than intellectual enlightenment, and were particularly important for allowing a chaperoned place for young men and women to court.

Contrary to many depictions of life on the frontier, there was much socializing that went on among homesteaders and in the towns. Any holiday was cause for celebration, a picnic, a fair, or a festival. The Fourth of July was usually the biggest celebration of the year, and the goings-on were elaborate. There were competitions, bands, parades, and exhibits. Competitions might be horse races, foot races, bicycle races, buggy and chariot races, boxing and wrestling matches, pulling contests with horses, mules and oxen, baseball games, and log-rolling contests.

Another occasion for get-togethers was bees – sewing bees, quilting bees, husking bees. Homesteaders would gather to raise a barn or a house, help with the canning, baptize, marry, and bury. With the exception of funerals, most of these gatherings required a dance before or after.

Where there was a violin on the frontier, there was a dance. One musician noted that playing his violin was a much more profitable way to earn a living than digging for gold. Dances were held everywhere in the West for every reason or no reason, and they often went on until sunrise. In the mining towns and cow towns where women

The Spanish missionaries of California and the Southwest were well-organized and persistent. The ruins of the mission they founded at San Juan Capistrano in California in 1777 still stand (*facing top*). The old adobe church is the oldest surviving building in California.

San Juan Capistrano (*facing bottom*) was founded by Father Junípero Serra, an energetic and able leader. The large,

seven-domed church built at the mission between 1797 and 1806 was destroyed by an earthquake.

Pioneer settlers gather to celebrate the Utah jubilee in Salt Lake City, 1897 (*above*).

Women were scarce on the frontier. Here (*below*) men dance with each other somewhere in Texas around the turn of the century.

were scarce, the men would dance anyway, and trade off playing the female part of the dance.

Entertainment in the mining towns and cow towns was usually ongoing, 24 hours a day, and of a more sordid type. Gambling was a primary form of entertainment, and also a primary way to lose one's wages. Dance halls, called hurdy-gurdy houses, were usually thinly veiled brothels. Every mining town seemed to have its opera house, built by the mine owner who had struck the biggest vein of gold or silver. The fare in the opera house consisted of actual operas, plays, melodramas, musicals, Shakespeare, variety acts, magicians, dancing girls, singers of every description, and preachers, with the dancing girls and variety acts predominating. Such world-renowned figures as Oscar Wilde and Sarah Bernhardt toured the mining camps of the West, performing in the opera houses. Wilde claimed the miners of the frontier West were the best audience he ever had.

The stages of the West produced many famous figures. Among the best-known was Lotta Crabtree, known as Little Lotta. Lotta was raised in a theatrical family and started acting as a child. Under the critical and encouraging eye of her mother, she became one of the best-loved actresses of the time.

DIME NOVELS AND WILD WEST SHOWS

Books, magazines, and newspapers were treasured by those pioneers who could read. Shakespeare and the Bible were the staple items in most literate households. Illustrated weekly news-

A view of the saloons and disreputable places of Hazen, Nevada, in 1905 (*top left*).

The girls of Hovey's Dance Hall in Clifton, Arizona, pose for their picture in 1884 (*bottom left*).

papers such as Horace Greeley's Weekly Tribune and Harper's Weekly were sparsely distributed in the West, and would be passed around, read, and re-read until they fell apart.

Horace Greeley was the author of the slogan, "Go West, young man!" The editor of the New York Tribune created this slogan after a trip to California. Every detail of the trip was written down and eventually made it into one of his publications. Greeley's accounts were almost as romanticized as the dime novels, and he praised the West as the land of opportunity.

The publishing medium that attracted the largest following and created heroes out of such men as Wild Bill Hickock, Buffalo Bill Cody, Wyatt Earp, and Bat Masterson, was the dime novel. These cheaply printed, romanticized fictions of life in the West portrayed larger-than-life villains and heroes that fired the imaginations of the whole country.

Buffalo Bill Cody became the most enduring and celebrated of the dime novel heroes. A dime novelist named Edward Z.C. Judson, who wrote under the pen name of Ned Buntline, met William Cody while traveling in the West. Cody was young, good-looking, and adventurous – just the hero Buntline needed. After the publication and incredible success in 1869 of Buntline's Buffalo Bill, the King of Border Men (still in print in 1928), Cody went on stage. The

Gathered around the kegs at Kelley's saloon, The Bijou, at Round Pond, Oklahoma Territory, in 1894 (*top right*).

An Arizona poker party, al fresco at John Doyle's ranch (*bottom right*). Doyle, Judge Brown, and the Professor are at play, 1888.

Cowboys take a break to
play hearts on the Three
Circle Ranch, Texas, in
1901 (*above*).

Rip-roaring fun in Butte
City, Montana, 1896
(*right*).

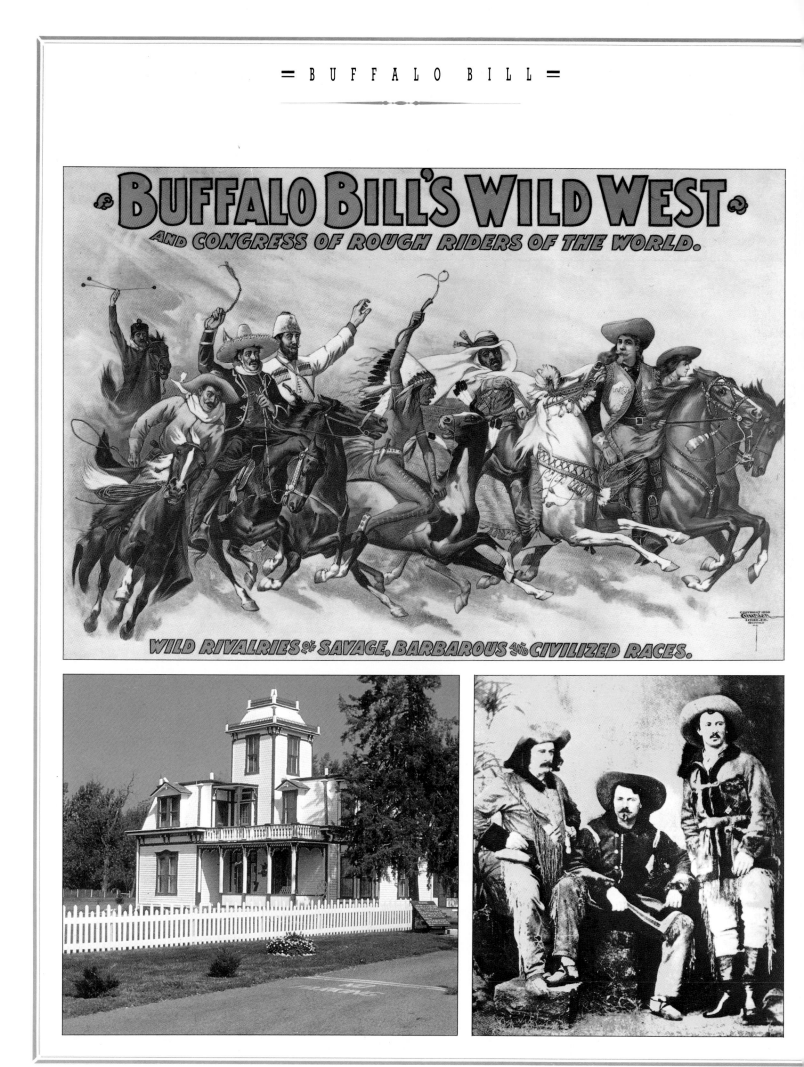

An advertising poster for Buffalo Bill's Wild West Show from around 1898.

Buffalo Bill's home on the ranch (*facing bottom left*) still survives as a state park in Nebraska.

The dime novels and melodramatic plays of Ned Buntline contributed to the romanticized view of Western life. Here (*facing bottom right*) Buntline (left), Buffalo Bill (center), and Texas Jack (right) pose in the costumes they wore while performing Buntline's drama *Scouts of the Prairie*.

Buffalo Bill poses with his Indian chiefs around 1894 (*above*). From left to right are: Spotted Tail, Crow King, American Horse, Chief Gall, Red Cloud, Crazy Head, Red Shirt, and Rain-in-the-Face.

Buffalo Bill returned to his Scout's Rest Ranch (*left*) in Nebraska whenever he could spare the time. The ranch bred shorthorn and Hereford cattle as well as horses.

frontiersman was a natural promoter, and soon after created the first Wild West show.

Buffalo Bill's Wild West Show toured the world for more than 20 years, and made Bill Cody a millionaire many times over. Unfortunately, he didn't have a head for business, and also found himself in bankruptcy over and over again. Imitating the success of his spectacular show, many of the men who had worked for him, such as Deadwood Dick, Pawnee Bill, Diamond Dick, Idaho Bill, and Dr. W.F. Carver, went on to form their own shows. Dozens of smaller shows appeared, usually sorely disappointing to their audiences. Pawnee Bill was the only promoter whose show came close to Buffalo Bill's. When Cody was close to bankruptcy in 1908, they combined their shows. Pawnee Bill's wife Mae Lillie was a sharpshooter whose act was similar to Annie Oakley's.

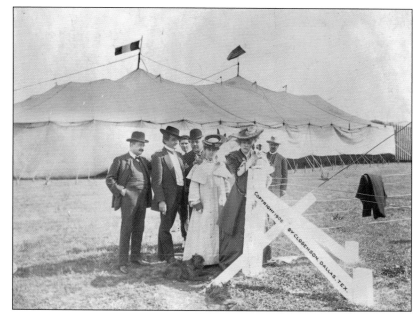

Hurdy-gurdy girls (*top left*) entertain at a saloon in Virginia City, Nevada, in 1865.

Sarah Bernhardt and her entourage (*left*) pose in front of a tent theater in Dallas, 1906.

A poster advertising French actress Sarah Bernhardt's American tour of 1906 (*above*).

Author Colonel Prentiss Ingraham kept the Buffalo Bill legend alive for years, traveling with Cody in his show and writing more than 80 novels about the one-time Pony Express rider and buffalo hunter.

Other heroes immortalized by the dime novels were Kit Carson, the Texas Ranger Big Foot Wallace, Calamity Jane, and Billy the Kid.

Author Bret Harte was another Westerner whose favorite subject was gamblers who always straddled the fence between conning the innocent out of hard-earned wages and gallantly saving the beautiful damsel in distress. Cavalryman Charles King immortalized the U.S.

Horace Greeley, influential editor of the *New York Tribune* (*top left*), was deeply interested in the Westward movement, giving it extensive coverage.

Actress Lotta Crabtree (1847–1924) posed for this daring photo (*bottom left*) in 1868.

The staff of the *Daily Reporter* in front of their office at Corinne, Boxelder County, Utah Territory, in 1869 (*middle left*).

Flamboyant Oscar Wilde (*top right*) went on a lecture tour of the West in 1879. Holding a white lily in his hands, he spoke to his audience of miners and ranch hands about the ethics of art. He later claimed they were the best audience he ever had.

The interior of the famed Crystal Palace Saloon, Tombstone, Arizona, in the 1880s (*bottom right*).

Gordon W. Lillie, better known as Pawnee Bill (*above left*), started his Historic Wild West Show in 1888; in 1894 the show toured Europe. From 1909 to 1913, his show merged with Buffalo Bill's.

The romantic West quickly became part of American folklore. This sheet-music cover (*top right*) for a song called "Bury Me Not on the Lone Prairie" was published in 1907.

Novelist Owen Wister (1860–1938) (*bottom right*) wrote one of the most enduring novels of the West, *The Virginian.* Published in 1908, the novel features a mail-order bride, a laconic hero, and a

Army cavalryman in dozens of tales of brave troopers fighting evil Indians and marrying the colonel's daughter. There were many of these authors, who captured the imagination of the American public and created the myth of the American West that still survives today.

Some of the dime novel heroes went from the printed page onto the silver screen. Both Tom Mix and Will Rogers (then called the Cherokee Kid), were skilled cow hands who could rope and ride anything. They found themselves in a rodeo show in Madison Square Garden in New York City. From there Rogers went on to become a rope-twirling star of the Ziegfeld Follies, a movie actor, and humorous writer. Mix became a star of the silent movies.

There were plenty of women heroes to entertain the folks back East and in Europe. Annie Oakley was one of the most enduring and popular stars of the Wild West Show. Her father died when she was very young. At the age of ten she was out shooting birds and small game to keep her family fed, and was soon selling the overflow to neighbors and a local hotel.

In 1879, when Annie was 19, a shooting match was set up between herself and professional marksman Frank Butler. She trounced Butler and walked away with $100. A year later they were married, and

climactic gunfight between the hero and the villain. It also has one of the best lines ever written in a Western novel: "When you call me that, smile."

Annie Oakley, the stage name of Phoebe Ann Moses (1860–1926) (*facing left*), was named Little Sure Shot by Sitting Bull. She toured with Buffalo Bill for seventeen years.

A former Wild West show performer, Tom Mix (*facing right*) made dozens of short cowboy films. The simple, virtuous characters he played helped create the romantic myth of the cowboy that persists to this day. This scene is from *Rough Riding Romance* (1919).

toured with their own show, called Butler and Oakley. In 1885 they signed up with Buffalo Bill's Wild West Show, and for 17 years toured North America and Europe.

Annie was petite, prim, and pretty. While her stage character was brash and heroic, in private she was a quiet, thoughtful person who enjoyed needlepoint. When the Sioux Chief Sitting Bull met her, he made her an honorary member of the tribe, and gave her the name "Little Sure Shot." She was presented to royalty all over Europe, including Queen Victoria.

Annie Oakley and Frank Butler lived a public life for many years. Annie died in 1926, a few years after retiring, and Frank died a few years later.

As the Wild West shows faded, the rodeo took over, spawning many stars of its own. "The Greatest Cowgirl on Earth" was Lucille Mulhall. Her rodeo act was to rope eight horses with one throw of the lariat. Legend has it that when Teddy Roosevelt visited her ranch, she amazed him by roping a coyote. Tillie Baldwin was a champion cowgirl trick rider, and the only woman bulldogger in the world. Bertha Blancett was the "champion lady bronco buster of the world," and became a Hollywood stunt rider.

INDEX

Figures in italics refer to illustrations.

A

Abilene, Kansas, 43, 44, 112
actresses, 131, *136, 137*
Adair, John G, 51
adobes, *14, 15, 22*
agriculture *see* farming
Alabama, *23*
alcohol, 7
Alkali Lake, Nevada, *80*
American Express Company, *88*
American Fur Company, *31, 39*
American Horse, *13*
Anasazi civilization, *14–15*
Anderson, "Bloody Bill", 104
Apache Indians, *9, 10, 11, 23,* 79, *79,* 82, 90
Apache Pass, Arizona, *79*
Apache rancherias, *82*
Arapaho Indians, 36
architecture, *35, 55*
Arizona, *20, 45,* 76, 79, *81, 97*
Arkansas River, 32, *38*
army *see* United States Army
army forts, *9, 24, 31, 35,* 36, *38–9,* 40, *41,* 43, *50, 53, 73, 74, 77, 83*
Arrow Maker, *20*
arrows *see* bows and arrows
Arthur, Chester A, *President, 114*
artists, *23–4, 63, 75, 89*
Ashley, William H, 33, *33*
Aspen, Colorado, 59–60, 63
Assembly Hall, Salt Lake City, *22*
Assiniboin Indians, *23*
Atchison, Topeka and Santa Fe Railroad, 65
Astor, John Jacob, *39*

B

Baby Doe *see* Tabor, Elizabeth McCourt Doe
Baldwin, Tillie, 139
Bandelier, Adolph, *15*
banking, *56*
barbed wire, *54*
Bean, Roy, *113*
Bear Flag Rebellion (1846), 76
bears *see* grizzly bears
beaver, 26, 28, *39*
Beaver Head River, Montana, *93*
Becknell, William, *38*
Beecher's Island, Battle of (1868), 77, 79
Bent's Fort, Colorado, 36, *38–9, 74*
Bent, Charles, *39*
Bent, William, *39*
Benton, Thomas Hart, 76, *76*
Bernhardt, Sarah, 131, *136*
Big Foot, *Chief,* 12, *12, 13*
Big Soldier, *Chief, 24*
bigamy, *19,* 22
Bignon, Joe, *115*

Billy the Kid, 53, 107–8, *108*
Bird Cage Theater, Tombstone, *115*
Bisbee Massacre, *118*
Bismark, South Dakota, 29
bison, *11*
Black Canyon, Colorado, *80*
Black Hills, Dakota, *13,* 61, *83*
black regiments *see* Buffalo soldiers
Blackfeet Indians, *24,* 41, *41*
blacks, *44,* 103
    see also Buffalo soldiers
Blancett, Bertha, 139
boarding houses, 66
Bobtail mine, Colorado, *69*
Bodmer, Karl, *24, 27,* 29, *41*
Bonney, William *see* Billy the Kid
books, 131–2, *135,* 136
Borginnis, Sarah, *122,* 124
Boulder, Colorado, 63
bourgeois house, Fort Union, *39*
bows and arrows, *10, 33*
branding, *45,* 51, 53
Bridgeman, John, *13*
Bridger, Jim, 28, *31,* 36
bridges, *94–5*
Bronaugh, Warren C, 105
brothel madams, 124–5
    see also prostitutes
Brown, Aaron, 90
Brown, DRC, 63
Brown, James Joseph, *66*
Brownsville, Texas, *122*
Buchanan, James, 76
buffalo, 7–8, *8,* 26, 36, *39*
Buffalo Bill *see* Cody, Will
Buffalo Bill's Wild West Show, 98, *98,* 112, *135,* 136, *138,* 139
Buffalo Pan-American Exposition, *126*
Buffalo soldiers, *50,* 74, *75,* 76
Bullion, Laura, 110
bullwhackers, 93
Buntline, Ned, 98, 132, *135*
Burch, Jim, 90
Bureau of Indian Affairs, *77*
burial customs, *13*
Burke, Clinton, 126
Burke, Mrs ME *see* Calamity Jane
Butler, Frank, 138–9
Butler, James *see* Hickock, "Wild Bill"
Butte City, Montana, *133*
Butterfield, John, *88,* 89, 90
Butterfield Overland Mail, 89
Butterfield and Watson Express Company, *88*

C

Calamity Jane, *124,* 125–6, *126*
California, 33, 35, 36, 40, 76, *81,* 88, *95*
California Gold Rush, 19, 56, 59, *62*

California Stage Company, 90
camp followers, 124
Camp Mohave, Arizona, *81*
Canada, 12, *23,* 28
Canary, Martha *see* Calamity Jane
Canyon de Chelly, Arizona, *81*
Canyon Diablo, Arizona, *94*
capital punishment, *73,* 74, *110, 112, 118*
Carey, "Laughing Sam", 108
carrier pigeons, 26
Carson, Kit, 36, *36,* 40, 76
Carson Valley, Nevada, *62*
Cassidy, Butch, 108, 110
Cataldo, *Father* Joseph, *18*
Catholic missionaries, *14, 18,* 35, 128, *131*
    see also missionaries
Catlin, George, *23*
Cattle Annie, 122
cattle breeding, 51, 55
cattle drives, 43–4, *43,* 45, *45–6,* 48, 49, *54, 56,* 57
cattle prices, 43
cattle ranching, *42,* 43–5, 48–9, *49–50,* 51–7, *53, 54, 55, 56,* 82, 113
cattle rustling, 53, 55, 57
cattle wars *see* range wars
Cavalry regiments, *12, 50, 73, 75*
Central City, Colorado, *59, 61,* 63
Central Overland and Pike's Peak Express Company, 90, 91, *92*
Central Pacific Railroad, *94,* 100, *101*
Chaco Canyon, New Mexico, *14*
Charbonneau, Toussaint, 29
Cherry Creek, Colorado, 59
Cheyenne Indians, 36, 76, *77,* 79, 85–6
Cheyenne River, South Dakota, *13*
Chicago, Illinois, 48
children, *9, 16,* 120, *120*
children's games, *20*
Chinese immigrants, *95,* 101
Chiricahua Apaches, *9, 11*
Chisolm, Jesse, 43–4, *43*
Chisolm Trail, 43–4, *43*
Chisum, John, 51, 53, 108
Chisum, Sally, 53
Choctaw Indians, *23*
Church of Jesus Christ of Latter-day Saints *see* Mormons
churches, 121, *127*
    see also religious buildings
Cimarron Desert, *38*
Civil War, 40, 43, 49, 53, 55, 65, 72, 73, 76–7, 83, 90, 101, 103, *103,* 104
Clanton gang, *115*
Clark, William, 28–9, *28*
Clear Creek, Colorado, 59
Clements, Manning, 103
cliff dwellings, *14*
Clifton, Arizona, *112*
climate, 28, 35, 45, *49,* 70

California Stage Company, 90
Cochise County Court House, Arizona, *115*
Cody, "Buffalo Bill", 97–8, *97–8,* 132, *135,* 136–7
Coffeyville, Kansas, 106, *107*
Colorado, *38, 58, 63,* 70, *77, 81, 93, 98,* 123
Colorado River, *20, 78*
Colter, John, 28, *35,* 40–1
Colter's Hell, *35,* 41
Columbia River, *30,* 32
Commanche Indians, 35
communications, 28, 59, 66, 88–93, 96–8
    see also transportation
Comstock mine, Nevada, *68, 69*
Concord coaches, 91
Conestoga wagons, *87*
Congress *see* Federal Government
conquistadors, *14*
construction engineers, *94–5, 98,* 100, 101
Continental Divide, 28, 33
Cook, P, *76*
coolies *see* Chinese immigrants
Coronado, Francisco, *14*
Corpus Christ, Texas, *72*
Corinne, Utah, *137*
Cortina, Juan, 55, *55*
Council Bluffs, Iowa, 101
court martials, 73
cowboys, *42,* 43–5, *43, 44,* 45, *45–6,* 48, *49–50,* 53, *133*
Crabtree, Lotta *see* Little Lotta
cradling, *68, 69*
craft work, *10*
Crazy Horse, *Chief, 13*
Creede, Colorado, *61,* 116
Crested Peak, California, *94*
Cripple Creek, Colorado, *61*
Crocker, Charles, 100, 101
Crook, George, *9,* 79, 82–3, *82, 83,*
Crow Indians, 40–1
Crystal Palace Saloon, Tombstone, *137*
cultural societies *see* lyceums
Currier and Ives, *6*
Curry, Kid, 108, 110
Custer, George Armstrong, 71, 79, 83, *84,* 85–6

D

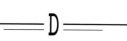

Dakota Indians, *24*
Dakota boom, 7
Dallas, Texas, *136*
Dalton brothers, 106, *107,* 112
Dana, Charles, 89
dancing, 129, 131, *131*
    see also Indian dances
Davis, Andrew Jackson, 57
Davis, Erwin, 57
Deadwood, South Dakota, 68, 92,

92, 93, 113, *113*, 126
death penalty *see* capital
  punishment
Deer Lodge, Montana, 56–7, *56*
deforestation, 26, *61*, 63
Dennis, William, 96
Denver, Colorado, 65, 66, *66*, 90, *92*,
  116, 124–5
desertion, *73*, 74
DHS Ranch, Montana, 57
dime novels, 132, *135*, 136
Dine *see* Apache Indians
Dinsmore, William, 89
diseases, 7, *29*
Dodge, Grenville M, 100–1, *101*
Dodge City, Kansas, 116, *116*, 117,
  117
Doolin gang, 112
Doyle, John, *132*
drag *see* point and drag
droughts, *15*, 57
Duffield, Frank, 122
Dull Knife, *Chief, 85*
Durango, Colorado, *59*
Durango and Silverton Railroad, *98*
dwellings, *10, 13, 14, 18, 25, 35*

E

Earp brothers, *111*, 113, *115*, 116–8,
  117, 118
education, 33, *70*, 103
El Paso, Texas, 89
electric lighting, 63
emigrants, *16*, 33, *62, 87*
  see also immigrants
entertainment, *20, 63, 66*, 67, *67, 115*,
  116, 128–32, *133–9, 137–9*
environmental destruction, 26, *61*,
  63, *68*
  see also land conservation
Episcopal church, *127*
Estes, Joel, 64
Estes Park, Colorado, 64
Evans, Jesse, 107
executions *see* capital punishment
exploration, *18*, 28–9, *28, 30*, 32–3,
  36, 40, 72, 76, *76, 78*, 80

F

Fanny Porter's Sporting House, 110
Fargo, William George, *89*
farming, *9, 15, 22*, 43, 82
Federal government, 12, *13*, 19, 22,
  26, 28, 89, 93, 94, 100, 101
federal grants, 90, *94*
fencing, *54*
festivals, 129
fire fighting, *129*
Florida, 12, *12, 79*
food and drink, 45, *46*, 65
food supplies, *17, 22*, 43, *56*, 57, *62*,
  65
Ford, Robert, 105

Forsyth, George A, 77
Fort Abraham Lincoln, Dakota, *83,
  84*
Fort Bayard, New Mexico, *73*
Fort Belknap, Texas, *53*
Fort Bowie, Arizona, *79*
Fort Bridger, Wyoming, *31*, 36
Fort Clatsop National Memorial,
  Oregon, *30*
Fort Concho, *50*
Fort Davis, Texas, *74*
Fort Dodge, Kansas, *38*
Fort Laramie, Wyoming, *31*, 77
Fort McKenzie, Montana, *41*
Fort Pierre, South Dakota, *24*
Fort Raymond, Wyoming, 40, 41
Fort Smith, Arkansas, 43
Fort Sumner, New Mexico, *53*
Fort Union, *27, 38, 39*
Fort Vancouver, 35
Fort Wingate, Arizona, *9*
fortifications, *22*
Four Bears, *Chief, 29*
Fox Indians, 24
Franciscan missions, *14*, 35
free land, *7*
Frémont, Jesse Benton, 76, *76*
Frémont, John Charles, 36, *36*, 40,
  76, *76*
frontier, the, 6–26, *6–26*, 28–41,
  28–41, 43–57, *42–57*
frontier towns, 43, 112
Fulton, Katie, 125
fur trapping, *18*, 28, *31*, 33, *33*, 35, 36,
  39, 40, *40*, 89

G

Gall, *Chief, 13*
gambling, *20, 115*, 116, 117, 118, *118*,
  121–2, 122–4, 132
Garrett, Pat, 53, 108, *108*
genocide, 7
geological surveys, 80–1
Geronimo, *9, 11*, 12, *12, 79*, 82
Geyser Basin, Wyoming, 28, *35*, 41
Gillespie, Henry, 59
Glidden, Jospeh Farwell, *54*
gold, 7, *7, 13, 18*, 19, 43, 56–7, 58–70,
  61, 62, 65, 68, 90, *93*
gold rush *see* California Gold Rush
gold stamping mills, *68*
Golden Spike National Historic Site,
  98, 101, *101*
Goldwater, Barry, *118*
Goodnight, Charlie, 49, 51, *53*
Goodnight-Loving Trail, 49, *50, 53*
Gore, George, 36
Grabill, JCH, *65*
Grand Canyon, Arizona, *78*
Grant, *President* Ulysses S, 76, 85
Great Basin, *20*
Great Salt Lake, 17, 35
  see also Salt Lake City
The Great Western

see Borginnis, Sarah
Greeley, Horace, 132, *137*
Green River, Wyoming, *78, 81*
Grierson, Benjamin Henry, *50, 75*
grizzly bears, 28, 29, 35, 36
grub stakes, 65
guerilla soldiers, 103, *103*
guides, 36, 70, *70*
  see also mountain men
Gulf of Mexico, 28

H

Hardin, John Wesley, 103–4
Harte, Bret, 137
Haslan, Robert, 96–7
Hauser, Samuel T, *56*, 57
Hays, John Coffee, 72, *72*
Hays, William, *39*
Hazen, Nevada, *132*
health care, *49*, 60, 121
Heith, John, *112*
Helena, Montana, 59
Hereford bulls, 51
Hickock, "Wild Bill", 112, 117, 126
Hidatsa Sioux Indians, *24*
hide hunters, 8, *8, 39*
hogans, *10*
Holbrook, Arizona, *10*
Hole in the Wall Gang, 108, 110
Holladay, Ben, 91
Holliday, "Doc", 117–8
Homestake mine, Dakota, *69, 93*
homesteaders *see* settlers
Hopi Indians, *14*
Hopkins, Mark, 100
horse breaking, *49, 73*
horse thieves, *102*
horses, *45, 49*, 55, *69*, 93, 96
hot springs, *35*, 41
  see also mineral springs
houses *see* dwellings
Hovey's Dance Hall, Clifton, *132*
Hudson Bay Company, 35, *35*
Humbolt River Canyon, Nevada,
  100
Hunkpapa Sioux Indians, *13*
hunting, *9, 20, 23, 33*
Huntington, Collis P, 100, *101*
hydraulic mining, *68*

I

Idaho, *18*, 29
illiteracy *see* literacy
immigrants, 7, *7, 95*, 101
  see also emigrants
Independence, Colorado, 59
Independence, Missouri, 88, 89, *89*
Indian agents, 40
Indian culture, 7–8, *9, 14–15, 23, 29,
  84*
Indian dances, *13, 14, 23, 29, 84*, 85
Indian Scouts, *9, 21*
Indian Wars, 11–12, *13, 18, 31*, 36,

40, *71*, 73, 74, *75*, 76–7, 79, 82,
  85–6, *85–6*
Indians, 7–8, *7, 9–15*, 11–12, *20–1,
  23–4*, 26, 28, 32, *33*, 35, 45, 72, 93,
  96
  see also reservations
Infantry regiments, 74
Ingraham, Prentiss, 137
Innocents, The, 57
Irish immigrants, 101
irrigation, *13*, 82
Ivers, Alice *see* Poker Alice

J

JA Ranch, Texas, 51
Jackson, David, 33
jails *see* prisons
James brothers, 103, *103*, 104, *104*,
  105–6, *105, 107*
Jefferson, Thomas, 28, *28*, 32
Johnson, George, *118*
Joseph, *Chief*, 11, *11, 18*
Joseph the Younger, *Chief, 18*
JR Ranch, Texas, *45*
Judah, Theodore, 100
Judson, Edward ZC *see* Buntline,
  Ned

K

Kansas, 43, *43*, 44, *44*, 85
Kansas City, Kansas, *44*
Kayenta, Arizona, *14*
Kearney, Steven Watts, *38*, 72, *74*
Keetley, Jack, 96
Kenedy, Mifflin, 55
Ketchum, "Black Jack", 108, *110*
Kilpatrick, Ben, 108, 110
King, Charles, 137–8
King, Henrietta, 55–6
King, Richard, 54–5, *54*
Kiowa-Apache Indians, *9*
kivas, *15*
Kleberg, Robert J, 55
Kohrs, Conrad, *56*, 57
Kohrs Pioneer Cattle Company, 57
Kruse, Augusta, 57

L

land grants, *94*
Langtry, Texas, *113*
Las Vegas, Nevada, *22, 38, 129*
law and order, 7, 21, 43–4, 51, 53, 55,
  55, 57, 70, 103–10, *102–5, 107–18*,
  112–8, 122
  see also Texas Rangers
Lawrence, Kansas, *88*, 105
lawyers, 60, 104
Leadville, Colorado, *58*, 59, 66, *66*,
  67, 70, 116
Leavenworth, Kansas, 90
Lewis, Gideon "Legs", 55

Lewis, Meriwether, 28–9, *28*, 32
Lewis and Clark Expedition, *18*, 28–9, *28, 30*, 32, 40, 88
Liberty, Missouri, *104*
Lillie, Gordon W *see* Pawnee Bill
Lincoln, Abraham, 101
Lincoln County War, 43, 108
Lion House, Salt Lake City, *19*
Lisa, Manuel, 40, *40*, 41
literacy, 28, 33
literature, *36*
Little Big Horn, Battle of (1876), 11–12, 79, 83, *83*, 85–6, *85–6*
Little Britches, 122
Little Lotta, 131, *137*
Little Pittsburg mine, Colorado, 66, *66*
Little Wound, *13*
lode mining, *69*
Long, Stephen H, 32, *32*, 33
Longbaugh, Harry *see* Sundance Kid
Looking Glass, *Chief, 18*
Loring, Fred, *76*
Los Angeles, California, 88
Los Pinos Indian Agency, Colorado, 70
Louisiana, 32
Louisiana Purchase (1803), 28
Loving, Oliver, 48–9, 51, *53*
LS Ranch, Texas, *42, 46, 49, 53*
lyceums, 129
lynching, *112*
 see also capital punishment

M

McCall, Jack, 112
McCarty, Henry *see* Billy the Kid
McCarty brothers, 108, 110
McDougal, Annie *see* Cattle Annie
Mackenzie, Ranald S, *50*
McLoughlin, John, *35*
McLoughlin House, Oregon City, *35*
McNelly, Leander, 55
Macy's store, 60
mail services, 59, 66, 88–93, *92*, 96–8
mail-order bridges, 7
Majors, Alexander, 93, *96*, 97
Mandan Indians, 29, *29*
Manifest Destiny policy, 76
mapping, 28, 32–3, 76, 80–1, 101
Marble Canyon, Arizona, *78*
Marent Gulch, Montana, *95*
Marshall, James, *62*
martial law, *114*
Massica Indians, *24*
Massmann, John, *63*
Masterson, Bat, 113, 116, 117, *117*, 118
Matchless mine, Colorado, 70
Maverick, Samuel, 53, *53*
mavericks, 53
Maximillian of Wied Neuwied, *Prince, 24*

Mechanics Corral, Fort Union, *39*
Medora, North Dakota, 92
Meek, Joe, 56
merchants *see* traders
Mescalero Apache Indians, *9*
Mesa Verde, Colorado, *14, 15*
Metcalf, Jennie *see* Little Britches
Methodists, 33
Mexican-American War (1848), 72, *72, 74*, 88–9
Mexico, 35, 72, *72*, 76
Midland, Texas, *50*
Miles, Nelson, *12*, 98
mineral springs, 35, *41 see also* hot springs
Miniconjou Sioux Indians, *13*
mining, 7, 58–70, *58, 61, 62, 65*, 68–9, *98*
mining shares, *65*
Mission San Xavier del Bac, Tucson, *129*
missionaries, *14, 18*
Mississippi, *23*
Mississippi River, 28, 29
Missouri, 76–7, 105–6
Missouri Fur Company, 40
Missouri River, 28, 29, 32, 33, *38*, 41, 91
Mix, Tom, 138, *138*
mochilas, 96
Mollie Gibson mine, Colorado, 60
Molly Brown House, Denver, *66*
Montana, 55, 56–7, *56*
Montezuma smelting works, 68, 69
Moore, Douglas, 70
Moore, Jim, 96
Mormon Lake, Arizona, *16*
Mormon Station, Nevada, 62
Mormons, 16–17, *16–17*, 19, *19*, 22, *22*, 36, 56, 88, 110
Moses, Phoebe Ann *see* Oakley, Annie
motion pictures, 138
Mount Agassiz, Utah, *81*
mountain men, 28, 33–40, *33–40*, 70
 see also guides
Mud Heads, *14*
mules, 82–3, *83*
Mulhall, Lucille, 139
music, *75*, 129, *129, 136*

N

Nanay, *Chief, 9*
Nauvoo, Illinois, 16
Navajo Indians, *10, 14*, 40
Navajo rugs, *10*
Ne-Mee-Poo *see* Nez Percé Indians
nesters *see* settlers
Nevada, 35, *81*, 100
New Mexico, *10, 38*, 40, *49*, 51, 53, *53*, 65, 72, *81, 84*, 108
New York City, 88, *91*, 116, 123
newspapers, *70, 114*, 116, 131–2, *137*

Nez Percé Agency, Clearwater River, *18*
Nez Percé Indians, 11, *11, 18*
nomads, *9, 20*, 82
Northern Pacific Railroad, *95*
Northfield, Minnesota, 105

O

Oakley, Annie, 138–9, *138*
Oglala Sioux Indians, 11, *13*
OK Corral, Tombstone, *111, 115*, 116, 118, *118*
Oklahoma, *120*
Old Tascosa, Texas, *121*
Omaha, Nebraska, *100*
OR Ranch, Arizona, *45*
Oregon, 33, *35*
Oregon Trail, *31*, 36
Orena, Nevada, *68, 69*
O'Sullivan, Timothy, *80, 81*
Ouray, *Chief*, 70, *70*
outlaws, 55, *55*, 103–10, *102–5, 107–18*, 122
 see also law and order
Overland Mail Company, 89
Overland Trail, 36
ox wagons, *68*, 93, *97*

P

Pacer, *Chief, 9*
Pacific Ocean, 28, 32
Pacific Railroad Act (1862), 101
Packer, Alfred, 70, *70*
Paiute Indians, *20–1*, 96–7
panning, *68*
Parker, Robert Leroy *see* Cassidy, Butch
Patee House, St Joseph, *90, 96*
Pathfinder, The *see* Frémont, John Charles
Patton, Harry, *129*
Pawnee Bill, *136, 138*
Pawnee Indians, *32*
Pecos National Monument, New Mexico, *14, 15*
Pehriska-Ruhpa, *24*
Peppin, George, 108
photography, *65, 80*
physical punishments, 73–4, *73*
Piegan Blackfoot Indians, *41*
Pike, Zebulon, 32
Pikes Peak Gold Rush, 59, *59*, 65, 66, 88, 97
Pine Ridge, South Dakota, *13, 86, 98*
Pinkerton Detective Agency, 105,112
Place, Etta, 110
Plains Indians, *77, 84*
Platte River, 101
Plummer, Henry, 57
plural marriage *see* bigamy
point and drag, *45*, 48
poker *see* gambling

Poker Alice, 122–4, *123*
politics, 7, *56*, 57, 65, 67, 70, 76, 77, 90
Polk, *President* James, 72, *72*
pollution, 26
Pony Bob *see* Haslan, Robert
Pony Express, 90, *90, 91*, 92–3, 96–8, *96*
Powell, John Wesley, *78*
preachers, 128–9
Prescott, Arizona, *73*
Preuss, Charles, 76
priests, *14*
prisons, 103, *112*
Promontory Point, Utah, *100*, 101, *101*
prospecting, *61*
 see also gold
 mining
 silver
prostitutes, *115, 119*, 121–3, 124–5
Pueblo, California, 65
Pueblo Indians, *10, 14–5*
Pullman cars, *100*

Q

Quantrill, William Clarke *103*
Quantrill's Raiders, *103*, 104, 105

R

Rabbit Tail, *21*
racial segregation, 74, 76
Racine Boy mine, Colorado, *69*
railroads, *8, 17, 38*, 44, *54, 90, 94–5*, 98, 100–1, *100–1*,
 see also transportation
Rain-in-the-Face, *Chief, 13*
ranch buildings, *55*
ranching *see* cattle ranching
range wars, 53
Rath & Wright, Dodge City, *8*
Raton Pass, California, 65
recreation *see* entertainment
Red Cloud, *Chief*, 11*1, 13*, 83
Red Dog, *13*
Red Shirt, *13*
relay stations, 93, 96, 97
religion, *15*, 16–17, *18*, 19, *19*, 33, *127*, 128–9, *129*
 see also Catholic missionaries
 missionaries
religious buildings, *15, 16, 18, 129, 131*
 see also churches
religious persecution, 16, 19
Remington, Frederic, *75*
remudas, *45*
rendevouz system, *33*
Republican Party, 76, *76*
reservations, 11, 12, *13, 15*, 77
rifles, *33*
Rio Grande, *72*

riverboats, 54–5
roads, 59
Rocky Mountain Fur Company, 33, 35
Rocky Mountains, *6, 20,* 28, 29, *32, 33,* 35, 59, 64, 76, *76,* 101
Rogers, Annie, 110
Rogers, Jennie, 125
E Romero Hose Company, *129*
Roosevelt, Theodore, *8,* 105, 116
Rose, Della *see* Bullion, Laura
Rose of Cimarron, 122
Russell, William H, 93
Russell Majors & Waddell, 90, *90,* 92, 97
rustling *see* cattle rustling

S

Sacagawea, 29
Sacramento, California, *62,* 92, 100
safety, *61,* 101
St Joseph, Missouri, *90, 91,* 92, 93, 106, *107*
St Joseph's Mission, *18*
St Louis, Missouri, 77, 89, 125
St Vrain, Ceran, *39*
saloons, 64, *64,* 65, *70,* 121–2, *121, 132*
Salt Lake City, Utah, 16–17, *16,* 19, *19,* 36, 88, *131*
    see also Great Salt Lake
San Antonio, Texas, 43, 72, 89, 90
San Diego, California, 90
San Francisco, California, 89, *91,* 93, 100, *100*
San Juan, *Chief, 9*
San Juan Capistrano, California, *131*
San Pedro Valley, Arizona, *114*
sanitation, 26, 63
Santa Fe, New Mexico, *75,* 89
Santa Fe Railroad, *38*
Santa Fe Trail, 35, *38–9,* 72, 89
Santa Gertrudis Creek, Texas, 55
Sauk Indians, *24*
Scarborough, George, 104
schools, *70, 120,* 121, *129*
    see also education
Scott, Winfield, *72*
Scout's Rest Ranch, Nebraska, *135*
Secrettown, Nevada, *95*
self-torture, *84*
Selman, John, 104
service industries, 64–7
settlers, 43, 45, *49,* 53, 72, 77, 88, 129
Seventh Cavalry, *12, 83,* 85–6
    see also Cavalry regiments
        United States Army
Shawnee Trail, 48
sheep rearing, *10,* 43, 53
Sheridan, Philip Henry, 76–7, *77,* 85
Sherman, William Tecumseh, 77, *77*
Sherman Silver Purchase Act (1878), 59, 63, 67
Shoe Bar Ranch, Texas, *45*

Short, Luke, *117,* 118, *118*
Shoshoni Indians, *20–1,* 29
Sierra Nevada, *20,* 61
silent movies, 138
Silks, Mattie, 124–5
silver, 7, *7,* 43, 58–70, *58, 59, 68, 114,* 116
silver dollars, 59
Silverton, Colorado, *59*
silverwork, *10*
Siouan Indians, *23*
Sioux Indians, 11–12, *13, 24,* 77, 79, 83, 85–6, *98*
Siringo, Charlie, 112
Sitting Bull, *Chief,* 11–2, *11, 13,* 86, *98,* 139
smallpox, *29*
    see also diseases
smelting works, *68, 69*
Smith, Jebediah, 33, 35, 76
Smith, Joseph, 16
Smith, Tom "Bear River", 112
Smithwick, Noah, 72
soil erosion, 26
South America, 110
South Dakota, 11, *12, 13*
Southern Pacific Railroad, *95,* 10
Spalding, Henry, *18*
Spanish influence, *14, 28,* 130, *131*
Spanish settlers, 22, 26
spinning, *10*
Spruce House, Mesa Verde, *15*
stampedes, 45
stagecoach stations, 90
stagecoaches, 72, 89, 90–2, *92, 93*
    see also transportation
Stanford, Leland, 100
Starr, Belle, *105*
Starr gang, 112
Storms, Charley, *118*
Story, Nelson, *56,* 57
Stranglers, The, 57
stray man, the, *53*
Stuart, Awbonnie, Tookanka, *56,* 57
Stuart, Granville, 56–7, *56*
Stuart, James, 56
Sublette, William, 33
sun temples, *15*
Sundance Kid, 108, 110
Sunday schools, *129*
Superintendent of Indian Affairs, 32
surveying *see* geological surveys
        mapping
Sutter, John, *62*

T

Tabor, Augusta, 66–7, 70
Tabor, Elizabeth McCourt Doe, *65,* 67, 70
Tabor, Horace Austin Warner, 66–7, *66,* 70
Tall Texan, the *see* Kilpatrick, Ben
Taylor, Elizabeth, 122
Taylor, Zachary, *72*

telegraph services, 59
temperance societies, 121
Tenth Cavalry, *50, 76*
    see also Cavalry regiments
        United States Army
tepees, *18*
Terry, Alfred, 79, 85, *85*
Teton Sioux Indians, *11, 24*
Texas, 43, *43, 46,* 48, 51, 53, *53,* 54–6, 72, 103
Texas Rangers, 55, 72, *72*
Texas Trail, *56*
theaters, 131, 136
Thompson, Cort, 125
Three Block Ranch, New Mexico, *49, 129*
Three Circle Ranch, Texas, *133*
Tilghman, Bill "Uncle Billy", 112, 117
Tombstone, Arizona, *111, 112, 114,* 116, 117, *118, 119*
Tonto National Monument, Arizona, *15*
trade goods, 29
traders, *18,* 35, 65, *65,* 66, 72
trading posts, 28, *33, 39,* 43, 45, *62*
traditional dress, *13, 21, 25, 29*
trail drives *see* cattle drives
transcontinental railroad, 100–1, *100*
    see also railroads
transportation *8, 17, 38,* 44, 54–5, *54,* 59, 72, *87,* 88, 93, *94–5, 98,* 100–1, *100, 101*
trapping *see* fur trapping
tree burials, *13*
tribal organization, *9, 10*
Tumlinson, *Captain,* 72
Tunstall, John H, 107, 108
Tuolumne County, California, *69*
Turkey Tracks Ranch, *49*

U

Uncle Dick Wootton *see* Wootton, Richen Lacy
Union Pacific Railroad, *100,* 101, *101*
United states Army, 7, 11–2, *12,* 18, 40, *50,* 72–86, *72–5, 77, 79,* 81–6, *98, 98*
    see also army forts
United States Geological Survey, *80–1*
US Postal Service, 90, *90, 91*
Utah, 16–7, 19, *21,* 35
Ute City *see* Aspen, Colorado
Ute Indians, *20–1,* 59, 70

V

Vasquez, Louis, *31*
de Vellombrusa, Antoine, 91–2
viaducts *see* bridges
vigilantes, 57
Virginia City, Nevada, *63, 65, 68, 127, 136*

W

wagon trains, 28, *38, 88,* 93
wagons, *68, 75, 87,* 93
Wakusasse Indians, *24*
Wallace, "Big Foot", 72
Wallace, Lew, 108, *110*
Walworth, James, 55
Washakie, *Chief,* 21
waste dumps, 63
water transport, 88
Watson, Ella, 122
weather *see* climate
weaving, *10*
Webner, Frank, *96*
Wells, Henry, *89*
Wells, Fargo & Co, *88,* 89, *89,* 91, *92, 93,* 117
Western Apache Indians, *9*
Western Quarter Horses, 55
Wheeler, B Clark, 59–60
Wheeler, George M, *80–1*
Wheeler, Jerome B, 60
whiskey, 65
White Bird Canyon, Battle of (1877), *18*
Wild Bunch, 108, 110, 112
Wild West shows, 98, *98,* 112, *135,* 136, *138,* 139
Wilde, Oscar, 131, *137*
wilderness areas, 26
Wilkinson, James, 28
Winsor, Anson Perry, *22*
Winsor Castle, Arizona, *22*
Wister, Owen, *138*
women, 7, *9–10, 16, 19–20,* 57, *105,* 110, *115, 119,* 120–6, *120, 122–4, 126,* 130–1, *132,* 138–9
women's suffrage, 121
Woolsey, King, 8, 11
Wootton, Richens Lacy, 64–5
Worden, Charles, *31*
Wounded Knee, Battle of (1890), 12, *12,* 83
wranglers, *45*
Wyoming, 33, 108, 121

Y

Yeellowstone National Park, Wyoming, 26, 28, *35,* 40–1, *56*
Yosemite National Park, 26, *26*
Young, Brigham, 16, *16–7,* 19, *19*
Younger brothers, 103, *103,* 104–6, *107*
Yreka, California, *62*

Z

Zion's Co-operative Mercantile Institution, *17*
Zuni Indians, *14*
Zuni Pueblo, New Mexico, *14*

═PICTURE CREDITS═